Revising Fiction

Making Sense of the Madness

by

Kirt Hickman

Quillrunner
Publishing
2009

Published in the U.S.A. by
Quillrunner Publishing LLC
8423 Los Reyes Ct. NW
Albuquerque, NM USA 87120

Printed in the U.S.A.

First edition

Book design by Michael Dyer, MOCA Book Design
Typeset in New Baskerville and Helvetica

This book is intended to provide accurate information with regard to the sub-ject matter covered. However, the author and publisher accept no responsibility for inaccuracies or omissions, and the author and publisher specifically dis-claim any liability, loss, or risk, whether personal, financial, or otherwise, that is incurred as a consequence, directly or indirectly, from the use and/or applica-tion of any of the contents of this book.

Cataloging-in-Publication Data is on file with the Library of Congress.
Library of Congress Control Number: 2009924645

ISBN 978-0-9796330-1-0

Early Praise for

Revising Fiction: Making Sense of the Madness

Revising Fiction ranks at the top of my list of "how to" writing books. Clear, concise, and exceedingly readable, it is better than any writing book to date. Hickman doesn't talk down to the reader. His goal, exceptionally done, is to help writers. Every writer should have this on his desk. Highly recommended.

> – Melody Groves
> author of award-winning *Arizona War*

Novelists who dare to proceed past writing a first draft soon learn the real work of creating a novel worth reading lies in the complicated process of revision. Kirt Hickman promises in the introduction of *Revising Fiction: Making Sense of the Madness*, to break the exhaustive list of revision concerns into a practical and effective approach. He does just that. As a writer, I've studied many books on revision. As a freelance editor, I've suggested many titles to clients. Kirt Hickman's *Revising Fiction* is now my number one recommendation to writers interested in making their novels marketable.

> – Keith Pyeatt
> freelance editor and author of the paranormal thriller *Struck*

Kirt Hickman has already helped an entire generation of New Mexico writers through his unique methods. He can help you!

> – Jonathan Miller
> author of *Rattlesnake Lawyer*

I have been writing and trying to edit for years. Editing is by far the hardest. I believe that Kirt's method is the most valuable thing I've learned. I've used it for everything I've written since.

> – Lela Belle Wolfert
> author of *Deception and Desire*

Revising Fiction is one of the best books I've read on the arduous task of revision. And I've read plenty. Unlike most books that take a cursory look at the revision process, Hickman rolls up his sleeves and digs into the grittiest aspects of examining fiction for flaws. Hickman is an engineer by training and it shows. His approach to revision is systematic, leaving no word unexamined... I've never found a better guide to the revision process.

– Rob Spiegel
president of SouthWest Writers, author of six books,
former owner/publisher of Chile Pepper magazine,
and former editor of two literary magazines

After you've toiled over your novel and had it critiqued by writer-friends who proclaimed it "good" and "enjoyable," it may not be polished. How do you know what's wrong with it or how you can fix it?

Kirt Hickman's *Revising Fiction* takes us through every pothole, cliché, awkward phrase, and how to solve each of them. His examples are smart and original, pithy and to-the-point. They allow you to think outside the box, and write more powerful scenes with more conflicted characters. He shows how strong verbs increase tension, actions, and even descriptions.

Revising Fiction entertains as it teaches, stimulates more ideas, and allows you to use more of your imagination. Unlike several other revision books, it's an enjoyable trip and worth the time.

– Eileen Stanton
Eileen's thirty-year writing career has included: humor columnist,
script writer, talk show host, creative writing instructor, and novelist

For Eileen Stanton, without whom
I never would have learned all this stuff.

P. 85

Each scene
must

1- Advance Plot
2. serve a purpose
3 advance character

Acknowledgments

A book like this can't be created by one person alone. It took the tireless effort of many to make *Revising Fiction* a reality. My thanks go out to all of you.

First, to Eileen Stanton, who wrote the critique of my first novel, *Worlds Asunder*, that launched me onto a journey that led to the publication of both *Worlds Asunder* and *Revising Fiction*. And, God willing, to many novels to come. I thank Eileen also for her critique of this book.

Next, to my network of test readers: Rob Spiegel, Laura Beltemacchi, Dollie Williams, and Abner Perez. Your comments helped make *Revising Fiction* the book I imagined it to be.

To my editor, Susan Grossman, for ensuring that *Revising Fiction* is the best that it can be.

To Michael Dyer, for exceeding all my expectations for book and cover design.

To my peers at SouthWest Writers, for your constant moral and technical support.

To my wife, Lisa, for giving me the time and encouragement to pursue such an ambitious project. You mean everything to me.

To Nancy Varian Berberick for the wonderful Foreword.

And to God for blessing me with all the necessary talents and resources.

Contents

Part III The Little Stuff

Part IV Finishing Touches

Foreword

by Nancy Varian Berberick

Recently I had the good fortune to be asked by Southwest Writers to critique and edit Kirt Hickman's novel *Worlds Asunder,* a fast-paced, near-term science fiction story steeped in political intrigue and set on Earth's moon. Kirt, who presents his extremely well-received writing seminars for Southwest Writers, has now written the book you are holding in your hands, *Revising Fiction.*

I have been a writing instructor for five years, a freelance editor for longer than that, and a writer of fantasy fiction for more than twenty years. I've authored nearly three dozen short stories as well as eleven novels, two of which became bestsellers. As you might imagine, I have spent a fair bit of time revising my fiction. This is the part I look forward to, for after the last word of the first draft is written, after I have set a manuscript aside to cool for a few days and then returned to it with a fresh mind, I am eager to begin the revision.

Red pen in hand, tea steaming in the mug, I can now view the manuscript as a whole, the sum of all those parts I've been putting together for weeks if it's a short story and for close to a year if it's a novel. Now I have the chance to refine my prose, enlarge my characters, expand the setting. I tinker with the plot and deepen the theme to make sure that this story or novel is the best it can be. My readers deserve no less.

Neither do yours.

If you don't have the opportunity to attend one of Kirt's writing seminars, not to worry. In *Revising Fiction,* Kirt has not only offered the collected wisdom of those seminars, he's provided exercises at the end of each chapter to help the writer on his or her way through each major step of creating a novel — from research and character creation to world building and so much more. *Revising Fiction* is not a mere primer on how to revise your novel — *Revising Fiction* is the kind of book writers read often, and often for pleasure.

And so when you find yourself at that intersection of Where Do I Go Now and How Do I Get There From Here, take this book from your shelf and enjoy some "hail fellow well met" for the journey.

Nancy Varian Berberick
Albuquerque, NM

Nancy Varian Berberick is the author of eleven novels, among them *Stormblade; The Jewels of Elvish;* and *Shadow of the Seventh Moon.*

Introduction

As the title implies, *Revising Fiction* is not so much a book on writing as it is a book on revising, on self-editing. It's based on the idea that the difference between bad writing and good writing is revision. Most authors, even best-selling ones, write problematic first drafts. Revision makes best-selling authors great.

Revising Fiction is the culmination of my personal journey to improve my own writing, a journey that began when I submitted my first manuscript, a science fiction novel titled *Worlds Asunder,* for its first professional critique. It got hammered. The critiquer sent back negative remarks on everything from characterization to scene structure to word choice, and rightly so; the manuscript was awful. I spent the next two years learning how to fix it.

The first thing I learned is that you can gorge yourself on the smorgasbord of tips offered in books on writing and revising or taught by speakers, teachers, writers, and editors in talks, workshops, classes, websites, and elsewhere. You'll discover an overwhelming mass of advice.

In every work of fiction, there's so much to be concerned about: plot, characterization, scene structure, setting, backstory, dialogue, and pacing. You must maintain suspense, portray your characters' emotions, show events rather than tell about them, make effective use of comparisons, and achieve consistency of style and voice. You must avoid passive voice, information dumps, repeated information, digressions, clichés, and unnecessary words and phrases. Finally, you must mind the details of grammar, spelling, word usage, punctuation, and format.

Whew!

How do you catch it all? How do you know when you've got it right? How do you even know where to start? *Revising Fiction* will answer these questions. In it, I'll break this exhaustive list of topics down into a practical, effective approach that you can use to improve your writing.

As you read this book, keep these things in mind: First, there are as many ways of writing, and as many ways of revising, as there are writers. No method works for everyone. Throughout *Revising Fiction*, I'll discuss the potential weaknesses you need to look for in your writing and I'll provide techniques to exterminate them. Furthermore, I'll present the techniques in the order I've found to be most effective. Consider each suggestion carefully and use those you find helpful. If you come away with nothing more than a list of things to be aware of, I'll have achieved my most important objective. I hope you'll come away with much, much more.

Second, there are no hard-and-fast rules. The rules this book teaches, such as "show, don't tell" and "use active-voice rather than passive-voice verbs," apply in the general sense to all forms of fiction. Nevertheless, numerous examples exist in which writers have broken the rules and gotten published. At times, you may wish, or even need, to violate the rules, but learn the rules first and abide by them the overwhelming majority of the time. Break them only to achieve a specific effect in your writing, never as an oversight in revision.

Third, as you progress through this, or any, revision process, edit for only one problem at a time. For example, consider editing for telling (summarizing events rather than showing them) and passive-voice verbs (e.g., "the car was stopped by Jon") as opposed to active-voice verbs (e.g., "Jon stopped the car"). Because these problems often appear together, you may be tempted to edit for both during a single pass through your manuscript. The problem is: They don't always appear together. When they do, you'll probably catch it. But when one appears without the other, you might spot it, you might not. In the end, you'll have corrected only some of the problems.

Those you miss may remain weak points in your manuscript until it's been submitted and rejected. Then it's too late.

Finally, the order in which you address the problems in your manuscript makes a difference. For instance, when you convert telling to showing, you'll create passages of new text. These passages might contain passive-voice verbs that you'll need to strengthen. If you edit for passive voice before you correct *tell*, you'll have to go back and look for passive voice again. On the other hand, when you convert passive voice to active, you'll generally rearrange a few words in the sentence. You're unlikely to create new passages of *tell* while correcting passive voice. Therefore, it's safe to edit for telling before you edit for passive voice, but not vice versa.

Throughout *Revising Fiction*, I'll use examples to demonstrate the various concepts. Most of the time, I'll offer a passage of writing that exhibits a particular problem or weakness, and then I'll discuss and correct the passage. These examples will not only allow you to see how it's done, but also to see that seemingly minor changes can make a profound impact on the quality of the writing. I've drawn examples from my own manuscripts, from critique submissions (with permission from the original authors), and, in rare cases, I've fabricated examples to illustrate my point.

At the end of each chapter, I offer exercises that will help familiarize you with the techniques presented in the chapter and to convince you of the value of those techniques.

The book also contains a self-editing checklist you can use to revise your own work.

Finally, *Revising Fiction* does not contain an exhaustive treatment of every writing topic. It attempts, instead, to lay down the basic principles and to present them in a way that makes them easy to understand and apply. I occasionally recommend additional sources that you may turn to for a more in-depth view — or sometimes just a different view — of a particular topic. My goal is for *Revising Fiction* to become your desk reference to self-editing, the one book that you, even as a published author, will reach for to prepare your fiction for the marketplace.

Part I

Before You Write

I stated in the introduction that *Revising Fiction* is a book on self-editing, not a book on writing. Nevertheless, the topics in Part I have a place within its pages. Indeed, you should do these things before you write your first draft, but if you don't, you must do them early in your revision process.

1

Your Concept

Theme

Your theme is your message.

When you sit down to write, particularly a work of book-length fiction, you probably have a story inside you that is clawing to get out. Sometimes it's a whole story, sometimes it's just an idea, a kernel of thought that intrigues you enough to put it onto paper. It may be a lesson for the reader to contemplate, a great idea for a hero or villain. Sometimes it's just a setting you've experienced and want to share through fiction.

When I began *Worlds Asunder,* I set out to write a series of science fiction novels that highlight the worlds, the planets and moons, in our solar system. We know a lot more about these worlds than we did in the days of Isaac Asimov, Ray Bradbury, and Arthur C. Clarke. Thanks to modern science, we no longer need to speculate about their nature. We know what these worlds are really like. That's cool, isn't it? Perhaps, but as a premise for a series of novels, it's not enough. Your story must be about something.

Science fiction themes often explore a question about a scientific advancement or trend in society. What if this or that technology (like time travel, teleportation, faster-than-light space travel, or genetic engineering) was developed to dominate the way we live our lives? What if some sociological trend (such as overpopulation, censorship, nuclear proliferation, or worldwide collaborative government) was extrapolated to its logical and frightening conclusion?

In the *Worlds Asunder* series, the question is: What if the various countries on Earth began to peacefully colonize the worlds in our solar system, and then one country claimed more than its fair share?

What is your story about? Jot it down. Put it in front of you. It will help keep you from digressing as your story evolves. If you've already written your first draft, determine the story's theme and revise your manuscript to bring out that theme more strongly.

World-Building

Jake Scranton shifted in the driver's seat of the old stagecoach as his team's fidgeting grew more violent. "Easy girls."

His partner, Buckshot Bill, gave him an uneasy glance — the company had already lost one coach in this canyon — and cocked both barrels of the shotgun cradled in his arms.

A tendril of dirt and pebbles trickled down the side of the sandstone cliff to their left.

Jake undid the clasp on his holster. He scanned the ridge, but saw nothing more until a rifle shot echoed across the canyon.

The bullet slammed Bill against the back of his seat. He slumped forward and fell from the stage. His shotgun tumbled to the floorboard and fired. The blast splintered the brake lever and Jake's startled team lunged forward.

Bad Bart and a dozen of his worst men rounded the corner behind them, whooping in anticipation. The thunder of hooves drowned the racket of the stage and its valuable cargo.

Panic coursed through Jake's blood as he fumbled the reins into his off hand and dialed the sheriff. *Come on. Pick up. Pick up.*

"Forget it," Buckshot said from the seat beside him. "You'll never get a signal way out here."

The approaching bandits rode their animals up to surround

the coach. All drew weapons of one sort or another. Bart raised his blaster. "Thou art mine!"

Where did this piece fall apart? When Jake drew a cell phone instead of his six-shooter? When Bill appeared beside him after tumbling from the stage? When the bandits' horses and guns became generic "animals" and "weapons of one sort or another"? Or when Bart raised a blaster and started spouting Shakespearean dialogue?

This story lost its credibility when you, the reader, detected inconsistencies in the world I created. Though this example is exaggerated, even absurd, it makes my point clear. Build your world carefully, completely, and with consistency, or your reader won't buy into it.

Regardless of your genre, you must know what your world will be like before you write. Ask yourself these questions:

1   What is your world like physically? What does it look like? What is the climate? What is the nature of the geology? The geography? Can you map it?

2   What are the moral codes of the time and place? What is society like? What are the predominant beliefs and values (even prejudices) of the various people who live there?

3   What is the economic state? Are people wealthy? Poor? Divided? How is commerce handled? With money? Barter? Information? Something else?

4   What is the domestic political structure? Does it work for the people (particularly for your main characters)? Why or why not?

5   What is the world political environment? Is it stable? Are countries at war? Who is the dominant power and why?

6   What is the predominant religion (or religions)? Are the people advanced enough to understand the differences among religion, philosophy, natural philosophy (science), and magic?

7   If there's magic, or any paranormal element, how does it work?

8   What is the level of scientific achievement? What are the preferred forms of transportation and communication? What is the state of medicine? Does your world have any unique technologies?

9   What is the day-to-day life of your characters like? How does it differ from that of your reader?

In science fiction or fantasy writing, you'll largely make this stuff up. For historical writing, or for a story set in another country or culture, you must do sufficient research to get these details right, but you *don't* have to do all of the research up front. I'll discuss this in greater depth in Chapter 5.

Either way, all the characteristics of your world and its background must mesh into a coherent whole. Keep this in mind as you write and revise your manuscript. If the details of your settings or characters are inconsistent with the world you've designed, your reader will pick up on it. He won't buy into your story. He won't read your book.

Exercises

1 Select a piece of fiction you're working on (a novel excerpt or short story). Determine its theme. Rewrite the piece to draw out or better emphasize the theme. Have someone read both the original and revised versions. Ask the reader which he liked better and why.

2 Select a piece of fiction you're working on (a novel excerpt or short story). Flesh out the world in which it takes place. Answer Questions 1 though 9 under World-Building. Do your answers mesh into a coherent whole? If not, why not? Correct any inconsistencies. Read your story with the answers in mind. If any story elements are inconsistent with your answers, correct those elements. Have someone read both versions. Ask the reader which he liked better and why.

2

Characters

You may have started with nothing more than a kernel of thought, but now that you've created your world, you should have a good idea of who your hero, villain, and prominent supporting characters will be. They must not be automatons. Your reader must buy into these characters as real people, with real goals, real motivations, real relationships, and real emotions.

Your characters must be multi-dimensional. They must have flaws as well as virtues. They must face internal struggles and external conflict. They must have past lives and prior relationships. Their previous experiences define how they view their world and their situation, and determine how they respond to their emotions.

You may choose to begin with a character archetype — a universal psychological and behavioral model — such as the loner, the teacher, the leader, the friend, the trickster, the knight, etc. Doing so will make your character's personality strong and identifiable. If you wish to delve into these fascinating character models, *The Writer's Journey: Mythic Structure for Writers*, by Christopher Vogler, and *The Complete Writer's Guide to Heroes & Heroines: Sixteen Master Archetypes*, by Tami D. Cowden, Caro LaFever, and Sue Viders, are both excellent references.

Employing an archetype need not — in fact must not — result in a stereotype. Your characters must be unique. Virtually any story idea you could conceive has already been told by somebody else. Yet if you tell the story through the eyes of a unique set of characters, the reader will experience it differently than she's experienced any other story. Use the tips in the following sections to individualize your characters.

Character Development

Consider each character in turn — not just your hero and villain, but your major supporting characters as well. The traits you assign here don't have to be spectacular or sensational. They can be small, even subtle, qualities. Your goal is to make each character a believable individual, not an incredible eccentric (unless, of course, you want him to be).

1   **Give each character a unique set of physical traits.**

These don't have to be scars and tattoos, the obvious choices for truly unique identifiers. Furthermore, these traits need not be unique among all humanity, just unique within the context of your story. If you have two or more similar characters, your reader may have difficulty keeping them straight.

Here are some example traits from *Worlds Asunder*.

Chase Morgan, NASA accident investigator
- He's fifty-eight years old, the oldest major character in the book.
- He's African-American. Chase isn't the only African-American in the story, but he's the only prominent character with this physical trait.
- He has a gray mustache and beard. Chase is the only major character with facial hair and the only character with gray facial hair.

Stanley Brower, chief of security at Lunar Alpha Base
- He has pale eyes that almost match his graying hair.

Dana McKaughey, Covert Armed Tactical Spacecraft (CATS) commander

- Her face is framed by shoulder-length, straight blond hair. She's the only blond in the book with short hair.
- Her eyes are "the color of the clear blue sky" (as characterized by her love interest, another CATS commander named Bill Ryan).
- She carries the subtle, alluring scent of bath oils (no perfume). Again, this is as characterized by Bill Ryan.

These physical characteristics need not be unusual. They're intended to individualize your characters, not to make them unbelievable. Nevertheless, the traits can be extraordinary as long as you account for them in a credible way through the character's background. The following are some of the more striking physical traits of characters found in *Venus Rain*, the sequel to *Worlds Asunder*.

Kelly Baker, nineteen-year-old planetary science student

- Her bleached hair is streaked with neon-pink highlights.
- She always wears her shirt open to expose her bra.

These characteristics stem from her rebellion against her single mother.

Colonel Chang, Chinese military, villain

- Parts of his raw face constantly seep blood. This comes from an old war wound that never healed.

2 Give each character a unique style of speech.

Each character should have a unique combination of dialect and vocabulary, based upon his personality, level of education, and upbringing, though these styles need not be widely disparate. For example, consider the following passage, quoted from three translations of the *New Testament*. A beggar sees apostles Peter and John on their way into the temple in Jerusalem.

> ... he began asking to receive alms ...
> Peter said, "I do not possess silver and gold, but what I do have I give to you ..."
>   — *From ACTS 3:3-6 (New American Standard Bible)*

> The man ... asked them for money ... But Peter said, "I don't have any silver or gold, but I do have something else I can give you ..."
>   — *From ACTS 3:3-6 (New Century Version)*

> ... he asked for a handout ...
> Peter said, "I don't have a nickel to my name, but what I do have, I give you ..."
>   — *From ACTS 3:3-6 (The Message)*

Though each of these passages says the same thing, each says it in the unique voice of the translator. The voices are similar. If these were the voices of three characters in a novel, they wouldn't sound strange together. Yet each has a distinct rhythm. If, while reading one translation, you encountered a verse from another translation, the transplanted verse would interrupt that rhythm.

Strive to achieve this with your characters. Make their speech rhythms different enough so that if a line of dialogue written for one character were attributed to another, that line would sound out of place.

3   Give each character a flaw that the reader can understand.

Your hero must be flawed. If you make her perfect, she won't be credible. Even if you manage to make her believable without building in a flaw or two, your reader won't be able to relate to her. Write about ordinary people in extraordinary circumstances.

Your hero's flaws often provide a source of internal conflict overlaid upon the external struggle provoked by the villain. Ratchet up the tension in every scene by exploiting your character's flaws to make her trials more difficult.

Here are some example character flaws from *Worlds Asunder* and *Venus Rain*:

- Chase Morgan's past mistakes, both personal and professional, cause him to look back on his life and consider himself a failure. Also, as a character in his fifties, he's not a paragon of physical strength and endurance. At times, this shakes his self-confidence.
- Director Jack Snider's ambition and focus on his own reputation often blind him to what's truly important.
- Stan Brower suffers from space sickness. He becomes incapacitated whenever he ventures outside the solid walls of Lunar Alpha Base. Of course, circumstances force him to go beyond those walls.
- Michelle Fairchild, an intern, is shy and inexperienced.
- Kelly Baker is rebellious, irresponsible, and has a tendency to make self-destructive decisions.

4   Give each character a special skill that she will find useful at some point during the story.

Special skills let your reader see into some aspect of life, some hobby or profession, that he might find interesting. In *Worlds Asunder*, Chase's skill, accident investigation, gives the reader a look into the investigative aftermath of a serious event. In *Venus Rain*, Kelly breaks into a laboratory storeroom and then uses a few basic substances, her chemistry know-how, and her impulsive creativity to get herself out of some tight spots. Her skill also allows me to present some hypothetical chemistry of planetary terraforming, which should be as interesting to the science fiction reader as it is speculative.

Introduce your character's skill early in the story, well before she needs to use it. Otherwise it will seem contrived — an afterthought you invented to get her out of whatever fix you put her into.

Present your character's skill at a technical level your reader can understand, and provide only information that is directly relevant to the events at hand. Otherwise the passage becomes a digression (discussed in Chapter 9).

5   Give each character a definable personality.

Is your character optimistic? Pessimistic? Grumpy? Funny? Flirtatious? Adversarial? What does she get fired up about? The environment? Animal rights? Poverty? Duty? Family? Honor? Love? Hatred? Vengeance?

Let's face it, without a definable personality and a passion for something, your character (your hero in particular) will be boring.

How does your character respond to frustration? This is an important decision. Your plot, which we'll discuss in detail in Chapter 3, consists of obstacles and events designed to frustrate your character's efforts. How will she react? Will she get angry? Resourceful? Determined? Depressed? Will she get even? Will she give up? (If she gives up, she's probably not your hero.) Will she seek help? Will she pray?

I'm not suggesting your character should respond to every situation in the same way, but people tend toward certain emotional reactions to frustration. Your character should too.[1]

6   Give each character an identifying line, mannerism, or prop.

Giving your reader something to associate with your

character besides a name will help her keep your characters straight. Here are some example character identifiers from *Worlds Asunder* and *Venus Rain*.

Lines:

> "You have to know what you're up against before you know what to do."

This is Chase Morgan's identifying line. Though he never actually speaks these exact words, they appear in his thoughts during the first scene of Chapter 1. Later, he speaks similar lines, such as, "We have no idea what we're up against" or, "Let's find out what we're up against." This provides a thread of character consistency throughout the book, an element of realism.

As another example, Jack Snider consistently uses auditory phrases like "Listen up" and "You hear me?" when he's agitated, which is most of the time.

Mannerisms:
Colonel Chang holds his right forearm level to the floor, with his hand cupped, rotating his wrist back and forth, back and forth. This nervous habit stems from the chemical explosion that ruined his face. It also broke his elbow. Physical rehabilitation required him to perform this repetitive motion to prevent the joint from fusing as it healed. Chang no longer needs the therapy, but the habit remains as a convenient way for me to show his emotions in a way that is specific to the character.

Props:
Don't restrict yourself to one kind of identifier per character. I not only gave Chase Morgan an identifying line, I also gave him a prop. In the beginning of the book, he

I E

almost always has a cup of coffee in his hand. David J. Corwell, one of my critiquers, made a note in the margin of my manuscript that said, "I think Chase likes coffee almost as much as the author does." I had to smile. David was right.

As the book progresses, however, Chase has less time for such trivial pleasures. By the end of Chapter 5, the coffee disappears completely until the next-to-last scene. The coffee gave me a subtle way to show that Chase has ventured beyond his comfort zone.

Another prop I want to discuss, because it became more versatile than I expected, is a cane carried by Victoria Powers, the president of the United States. She doesn't need the cane to walk, yet she carries it everywhere. She uses it as a status symbol or object of succor. She bangs it on the floor to get attention. She extends it in front of people as a way to stop them without her having to say a word. She lays the cane across her lap, grips it tightly when she's tense, and taps her wedding ring on it when she's nervous. When the burden of her office seems too much for her own legs to bear, only then does she use the cane to help her walk. The cane became a wonderful way to show emotion in a way that is specific to Victoria Powers.

Establish identifiers early, preferably the first time you introduce the character. Exhibit the identifiers every time the character appears in a scene.

7   Give each character virtues.

This is particularly important for your hero. Generally speaking, the reader must like her. Some authors can pull off a main character that the reader doesn't like, but not many. Even then, the reader must want the hero to achieve her goal. If the reader doesn't care, the book won't hold his interest.

No matter how many internal demons your hero has

to overcome, she must have at least one redeeming quality that your reader can latch onto and that makes him say, "I care. I hope she overcomes it all because she's worth saving."

In *Venus Rain*, the hero, Kelly Baker, is a mess. She's rebellious, promiscuous, and irresponsible. She lives life at odds with her single mother, dates an older man, wears her clothes and hair in a manner the reader might not approve of, enjoys a legal drug that she insists is benign, and subscribes to lust over love.

So why should the reader care about her? Because she has a couple of virtues that override this laundry-list of demons. First, she's smart. She goes to college and doesn't have to work very hard to understand the lessons. If she can turn her life around, she has the potential to do something great with it. Second, her irresponsibility ends when it comes to taking care of her little brother, Rod. Because their mother works constantly, Kelly has raised her brother since she was ten years old. When Rod gets into trouble, early in the first chapter, Kelly rushes to put her own life at risk to save him.

Give virtues to your other characters as well, including your villain. The villain rarely considers himself to be the bad guy. Whatever he does, he does for a reason. Sometimes it's just for personal gain, like the bank robbers in the old westerns. Often, however, he believes he's working toward some greater good, however warped that perception might be.

Virtues may not make your reader like your villain — you probably don't want your reader to like him — but virtues will help your reader understand him. Maybe your villain has a strong sense of loyalty, just to the wrong person, group, or cause. In *Venus Rain*, Chang is a military leader. He's loyal to duty. He follows orders. Because he's a military officer, the reader will understand this. It's not his fault his leaders have ordered him to do harm in the national interest. Of course, even with this understanding, the reader will want him to fail.

8   Know each character's backstory.

I can't stress the importance of this enough. As a writer, you must know the details of your character's backstory in far greater depth than you'll ever reveal in the pages of your novel. Your character's past has made him the person he is today. His past will determine his emotions, attitudes, and actions. And it will justify them to the reader. His past will make him real.

During *Venus Rain*, Kelly does a lot of maturing. She makes some decisions that get her into serious trouble and she begins to see the truth in the things her mother has told her over and over again but that Kelly has refused to listen to. Her mother, Amanda, realizes that her own priorities have been out of place, that she's neglected her family in pursuit of her job. In other words, each character takes steps toward understanding the other. The reader will expect Kelly and Amanda to eventually reconcile. One of the book's surprises is that they don't. Because they don't, the magnitude of the rift between these two characters must justify their failure to do so.

It's not enough for me to tell the reader that Kelly and Amanda had a series of fights, each of which widened the rift between them. I had to construct for myself what those fights were about, when they occurred, and how each changed the attitude of the characters toward one another.

It began when Rod was born and Kelly's father left the family. After the divorce, Amanda had to work constantly just to pay the bills. Kelly was supposed to take care of Rod, but she was too young to baby-sit responsibly. Her poor supervision resulted in an accident that cost Rod his right hand at the age of two. Though Amanda has never said so out loud, she blames Kelly for the accident, along with all the financial, emotional, and physical hardships it has caused over the years.

A year later, Amanda disappointed Kelly when work forced her to cancel Kelly's eleventh birthday party. Kelly's first crush, Neil Jorgensen, had planned to attend the party. Embarrassed by the sudden cancellation, Kelly couldn't face Neil. A short time later, the boy and his family moved away and Kelly felt she'd lost her first love. After a long string of similar disappointments, Amanda's canceling the party cost Kelly the ability to count on her mother for even the smallest of things.

This mutual loss of trust caused Kelly to become rebellious. She unconsciously sought ways to disappoint or anger her mother. When Kelly was fifteen, Amanda caught Kelly with a boy in her bed. Amanda found drugs in Kelly's room when Kelly was seventeen. At the time *Venus Rain* takes place, Kelly is nineteen and her bother is old enough to watch after himself most of the time. Although Kelly still lives at home for financial reasons, she's a legal adult and actively avoids her mother. Their relationship is no longer salvageable.

At one point, I even wrote the dialogue for each of these confrontations, though little of it appears in the book.

If you want your characters to come to life for your reader, you must know at least this level of detail about every aspect of their backstory. Get to the root of each and every character trait listed above.

Write a character biography. Focus on the aspects of your character's past that have defined her — that have affected her motivation and the decisions she makes later in life. This biography should be several pages long. Interview your character to flesh out any unclear or inconsistent points in her past. Get her to fill in the gaps in her history and character makeup.

9 Know how each character will change throughout the story.

The change your character makes, and the way that change comes about, is the character's arc. Provide an arc for each major character, not just the hero, but make the hero's arc dominant in the story. Give your villain an arc too, though his change may be from a bad guy to a dead or imprisoned guy.

I'll discuss character arcs in more detail in Chapter 3.

10 Make your villain stronger than your hero.

Don't make your hero's victory a foregone conclusion.

Characterization Pitfalls

Once you've fleshed out your characters, go back and revise them. Make sure you've avoided the pitfalls discussed below.

1 Make sure each character's personality is different from that of every other character.

You don't want all your characters to behave in the same way or talk like one another. They're people, not automatons. If each is like the others, none will seem real. And if your characters don't seem real, your reader won't care about what happens to them. Even if you've created a society that discourages individuality, your characters must be individuals, each with his own thoughts and ambitions.

2 Make your hero strong-willed.

It's hard for your reader to relate to a wimp or a pushover. If your hero doesn't care enough about his cause to assert himself to achieve it, why should the reader care enough to read about it?

Make your hero a doer, not a watcher. If he just stands by while somebody else solves his problems and overcomes his obstacles for him, he's not much of a hero. Your reader wants a hero who rises to the challenge, faces problems head-on, overcomes adversity, and either achieves his goal or becomes ennobled by his effort to do so.

In the early drafts of *Worlds Asunder*, Chase was too much of a watcher — not enough of a doer. To correct this, I rewrote every scene and took every opportunity to make him a doer.

One of many changes occurred in a vehicle pursuit scene. Chase and his companions, a handful of soldiers and security guards, must run for their lives after being ambushed by a large enemy force.

As I originally wrote the scene, Chase sat in a passenger's seat. He helped in his own way, by trying to call for help on the radio and by picking up a gun (as did several other characters) and shooting at the pursuers. But he wasn't driving. He wasn't in control. He was just one of the "several other characters."

In the rewrite, I swapped seats. With Chase at the wheel, his decisions matter much more than they did when he was just picking up a gun and shooting. Because the scene is told from Chase's point of view, the reader is now in the head of the character who matters most. It transformed the whole flavor of the scene.

This change may seem minor, but it makes my point. Put your hero in the driver's seat, literally and figuratively, at every opportunity.

3 Remove clichéd character traits.

Go back though your list of traits for each character. Have you created a dumb blond, a mad scientist, a brutish albino hit man, a crooked sheriff, or any one of dozens of character types that have been done to death in books and movies? Take your dumb blond and make her not dumb or not a blond (or maybe not a her). Make your mad scientist not mad or not a scientist.

Consider a western with a stereotypical crooked sheriff. He owns the town, rules by fear, accepts bribes from

criminal elements, and has the judge in his back pocket.
Yuck! Too clichéd!

When I find a clichéd character in my own writing, I
play "What if..." or "Suppose..." These words help me
brainstorm ideas to twist my character until he no longer
feels clichéd.

How might one twist the crooked sheriff to make
him more original yet still able to fill the same role in
the story?

Suppose he doesn't own the judge. Instead, he's char-
ismatic and has a talent for swaying a jury. That's a little
different, but not enough. He's still a crooked sheriff.

Suppose he's not the sheriff, but the deputy. Okay, so
is he in a position of sufficient power to serve his purpose in the story? That depends on what his purpose is.
If he's a minor character, he might be. If he's the main
villain, probably not, unless...

Suppose the sheriff's gone a lot, leaving the deputy
plenty of opportunities for corruption and villainy. But
why would the sheriff leave him in town alone so often?

Suppose the sheriff has frequent business away from
town, chasing bandits or talking to ranchers about a cat-
tle-rustling problem. *Suppose* the corrupt deputy stays
behind because he's afraid of horses. Somebody's got to
maintain order in town while the sheriff's gone. Right? A
fear of horses would make an unusual character trait for
a western lawman. As such, you must justify it through
the character's backstory. Of course, he could feign fear
as an excuse to stay behind and commit villainy, but a
genuine fear would generate much more interest.

Suppose he developed his fear when he fell off a
horse as a child. That could be his understandable
flaw, but it would have to have been a pretty severe
fall. *Suppose* the accident was so bad that it caused a
peculiar form of brain damage that prevents him from
remembering numbers. Ooh, I like that; it's original

and specific. I once saw a news story in which the victim of an accidental head trauma lost the ability to remember phone numbers. In this example, though, it would have to be numbers in general — there weren't many phones in the Old West. Of course, your deputy must be required to remember an essential number — a stagecoach arrival time, perhaps — at some crucial point in the story. That would make his unique trait important.

See how it works?

More subtly, do you have an otherwise-original character that exhibits a single trait that's a cliché for his character type? The brutish hit man who happens to be albino might fall into this category. Albinos are certainly rare, but in literature and movies, they almost always appear as brutish villains. Move this trait to a sophisticated good guy, maybe even the hero. How might that affect his life, the way people treat him, or his opportunities for social, political, or economic advancement? Is his society tolerant of such aesthetic differences? Does it hinder him in his quest?

Here I must make a distinction between realism and cliché. What if you create a ten-year-old boy who never cleans his room or a New York City cabby who drives like a maniac? Are these realistic or clichéd? Here's my test: Do most real ten-year-old boys live in dirty rooms, or do most keep them clean? I suspect the former. If so, a character with this trait is realistic. He should have some trait that's unusual for his demographic, however, so he doesn't feel to the reader like a cardboard cutout. If most *real* ten-year-old boys live in clean rooms but a high percentage of *fictional* ten-year-old boys are characterized by dirty rooms, a ten-year-old boy with a messy room falls into the realm of cliché. Apply the same test to the New York City cabby.

By contrast, are most sheriffs really corrupt, or are

they just portrayed that way too often? In this case, the latter is true. This is what makes the crooked sheriff, the dumb blond, the mad scientist, and numerous other character types clichés.

Apply this test to each of your characters. If you find a single clichéd trait in an otherwise-original character, one solution is to replace the trait with its opposite. Do what the reader won't expect. If this changes your story line, then change it you must. You don't want a plot that's based on a clichéd character trait.

4   Don't forget your secondary characters.

The waiter, the cab driver, the shoeshine boy, and other characters who appear fleetingly need not be fleshed out as completely as your main characters, but that doesn't mean you should leave them as cardboard cutouts. Give each a trait or two from the list in the previous section. Something unique. Something memorable.

Character Profile

Fill out a profile for each major character (your hero, villain, and any prominent supporting characters). This listing of important information will include the traits you developed above and other, more mundane details.

The profile in Figure 1 serves only as an example. Adapt it to include the things you think are important. For example, a friend of mine who writes mysteries always adds the question: If this character were to kill somebody, what would he use as a weapon?

Don't skimp on your character's background. Flesh it out. Many of the details in the profile will never make it onto the pages of your novel, but they're important nonetheless. The better you know your character, the more real he'll be to you and to your reader.

Put these profiles where you can see them while you write and edit your scenes. They will help you keep your characters consistent in both physical and emotional detail. If your character has

Character Profile

1 Name (including nickname, if applicable):
2 Gender:
3 Age:
4 Health:
5 Appearance (including unique physical characteristics):
6 Identifiers (including lines, mannerisms, and props):
7 Education or vocation:
8 Occupation:
9 Current job (including job title, company name, and duration):
10 Employment history (including jobs, company names, and time spent at each):
11 Boss and employees:
12 Economic status:
13 Marital status:
14 Family, children:
15 Parents' occupations:
16 Spouse's occupation:
17 Ethnicity:
18 Past relationships:
19 Current relationships:
20 Home (including location, size, and description):
21 Possessions (including car, electronic gadgets, sentimental items, and pets):
22 Recreation, hobbies:
23 Clubs and organizations:
24 Special skills or talents:
25 Skill deficiencies:
26 Tastes (including music, literature, art, food, etc.):
27 Religious beliefs:
28 Political beliefs:
29 Police record:
30 Sexual history and orientation:
31 Ambitions, desires, and long-term goals:
32 Fears and superstitions:
33 Prejudices:

Figure 1. Character profile, continued over

34 Favorite places (including physical and on-line locations, if applicable):
35 Astrological sign:
36 Personality (optimistic, pessimistic, grumpy, funny, flirtatious, adversarial, etc.):
37 Temperament (how your character responds to frustration):
38 Character flaws:
39 Habits, addictions, or vices:
40 Virtues:
41 Backstory:
      - Place where the character grew up:
      - Past triumphs:
      - Past failures:
      - Childhood traumas:
      - Earliest memory:
42 How will your character change throughout the story?

Figure 1. Character profile

blue eyes in the beginning of the book and brown eyes later (with nothing in between to account for the change), your readers will catch it.

Additional Resource

If you need additional help with character development, I recommend *Dynamic Characters*, by Nancy Kress. In *Dynamic Characters*, Nancy discusses how to inject character into every aspect of your novel.

Exercises

1   Select a piece of fiction you're working on (a novel or short story). Write down the character traits for your hero and villain. If your characters are missing any elements from the list given in the first section of this chapter, develop those elements. Complete a profile for each character. How might these new details impact your ability to portray the characters as individuals? Do the same thing for your prominent supporting characters (any characters who appear in your story on a regular basis).

2   Review your answers from Exercise 1. Is your hero strong-willed? Does your villain have a reason for doing the evil he does? Have you avoided the other pitfalls? If you answered "no" to any of these questions, use the "suppose" method to generate at least three ideas to correct each problem. Consider how these might affect the story. Incorporate your favorite ideas into your characters.

Make each character s
should have

1. Set of physical TRaits
2. unique style of speech
3. Flaws
4. special skill
5. definable personality
    IE: optimistic, pessimistic, Grumpy
6. identifying line, mannerism
    IE. something to associate ₹ your charact
7. virtues
8. Backstory
9. changes throughout story
10. villicen should be stronger

3

Plot

Some writers determine at least the skeleton of their plot before they write their first draft. Others begin with a character, a goal, and an obstacle and then let the plot develop from these as they write. Whichever way your plot evolves, at some point you'll have to answer this question: Is it any good?

Plot Basics

1 The elements of plot

One way or another, every story must have a beginning, a middle, and an end. You must introduce one or more characters and the circumstances surrounding the action. You must have conflict. And you must resolve the conflict. Together, these make up the three-act structure:

ACT I   =   Beginning   =   Setup
ACT II =   Middle   =   Conflict
ACT III =   End   =   Resolution

Always begin with a character, preferably a character the reader cares about. Give your character a goal. Make the goal personal and the stakes high. The higher the stakes, the stronger the plot.

Place a difficult obstacle between your hero and his goal. Someone or something must stand in your hero's way. This provides the source of conflict.

Finally, whether the hero achieves his goal or not, resolve the conflict in a decisive and satisfying manner. And — this is important — your hero must take the action most responsible for resolving the central conflict. In other words: Don't let some other character solve your hero's problem for him.

2 Cause and effect

Never lose the ever-important thread of cause and effect. Every event in your story must be the direct result of a character's actions (which must be driven by the character's motivations and objectives) or an earlier event.

Any event that doesn't stem from one of these causes constitutes author manipulation, which your reader will recognize. At best, the reader won't believe your story. At worst, he'll resent and distrust you for it. Either way, he won't read your book.

3 Life change

Your hero must go through a permanent, life-altering change during the story. If he doesn't, the stakes are either not high enough or not personal enough.

Mythic Structure

How should you set up the conflict and how should it play out? The answer lies in the mythic structure.

Joseph Campbell introduced the mythic structure as seventeen steps, or stages, of the story in *The Hero with a Thousand Faces*. Christopher Vogler presents the same structure as twelve stages in *The Writer's Journey — Mythic Structure for Storytellers*. James Scott Bell lists ten steps in his book *Plot & Structure*. I'll present it here in nine. It doesn't matter how you dice it, it's all the same structure.

Why are so many authors teaching mythic structure? Simple. It works. Ever since storytelling became an art form, the stories that have endured, generation after generation, have exhibited this structure.[1,2]

Rather than use *Worlds Asunder* as a case study — which might spoil the book for those who wish to read it — I'll refer to the popular films *Raiders of the Lost Ark* (Paramount Pictures), *You've Got Mail* (Warner Bros.), and *Shrek* (DreamWorks). I chose these movies because they're all excellent, they represent a wide range of genres (action-adventure, romantic comedy, and children's animated feature), and because you've probably seen them. If you haven't, rent them and look for the following checkpoints:

1   Ordinary life

Your story should pull the hero away from his ordinary life. Before it does, however, you must show the reader what that life is like. This will help the reader understand the impact the crisis will have on that life and on the hero. Show the reader what kind of person your hero is. Give her a moment to connect with him in a setting she can understand and relate to. Give her a reason to care about your hero.

Raiders of the Lost Ark reveals two different aspects of Indiana Jones' "ordinary" life. First he steals, um, I mean recovers, a lost golden idol from a dangerous temple. This shows him to be an adventurous character and promises plenty of action in the film to come. Then we see the mundane, academic life that undoubtedly consumes most of his days. We grow to like Indy because he's smart and courageous, and because he doesn't seek lost treasures for his own gain. He insists that the relics he finds be displayed in museums for the greater good of humanity.

In *You've Got Mail*, we see Kathleen Kelly's ordinary life both at home and at her bookstore, The Shop Around the Corner. We see how she interacts with her customers, especially the children. She likes kids, so we like her. At home, she runs to her computer for email from her on-line pen pal as soon as her boyfriend leaves the house. This shows her discontent with her current situation. For Kathleen, life change is around the corner.

In *Shrek,* the ordinary life of Shrek, an ogre, is shown during the film's opening credits, where he bathes in a mud hole and prepares a meal of slugs. These credits also show that he's deeply content with his life as it is, which creates some of the essential internal conflict: Shrek's resistance to change.

2   Story starting point

Something happens to change the course of your hero's life. Some authors refer to this as the "disturbance," the "inciting incident," or a "call to action." It may be something subtle or something catastrophic. Either way, it signals to the hero, and to the reader, that this is no ordinary day. The story's starting point should occur as early in the book as possible.

Army Intelligence pays Indiana Jones a visit. Hitler's men seek something in the Egyptian desert and the army needs Indy to interpret a cryptic communication about it. He identifies the Ark of the Covenant as the object of Hitler's search.

The new building across the street from Kathleen Kelly's bookstore is unveiled as her big-chain competition, the Fox Books Superstore.

Shrek finds a "Wanted" sign offering a bounty on fairytale creatures, including ogres.

3   Heeding the call

Your hero makes a decision or a decision is made for him. One way or the other, he leaves his ordinary life to embark upon whatever challenge the plot presents to him. After all, what kind of hero would he be if he didn't? Nevertheless, he should hesitate to jump in. If the decision to take the challenge is easy for him, the challenge isn't daunting enough.

Indiana Jones accepts the assignment. His only hint of reluctance is to make sure the Ark will, in fact, end up in a museum once he recovers it. He has no idea what dangers he will soon face.

Kathleen Kelly denies the implications that are obvious to everyone around her. She claims that the opening of Fox Books is a good thing — that the area will become a book district. But when Kathleen's weekly sales drop by twelve hundred dollars, the decision has been made for her. She must face the impact Fox Books will have on her business.

Shrek scares away a mob of bounty hunters and tries to continue his ordinary life. Then a host of fairytale creatures shows up at his home, having been sent there by Lord Farquaad. Shrek wants to get rid of them, so he decides to leave his home and confront Farquaad.

4   Allies and enemies

The hero leaves his normal life and enters unfamiliar territory. He discovers who his allies and enemies are and begins to learn the rules of his new world, new relationship, new case — whatever his new situation may be.

Indy's new "world" is his new quest: the quest for the Ark. He meets Marion (an ally) and Toht (an enemy) in The Raven saloon in Nepal, where Indy goes to seek the headpiece of the staff of Ra. There, he must learn who his friends are.

In *You've Got Mail*, the defining of Kathleen's allies and enemies takes place over two consecutive scenes, one in Kathleen's bookstore, the other at a dinner party. Many of Kathleen's customers seem to have gone over to Fox

Books, her employees worry about the store's closing, a loyal author expresses doubt about the Shop's future, and Kathleen comes face-to-face with Joe Fox (and realizes for the first time that he is Joe Fox). Throughout these scenes, Kathleen tries to assess the loyalties of the people around her.

Shrek barges into a tournament and confronts Farquaad. He fights all the knights before Farquaad sends him on a quest to rescue Princess Fiona.

Often, the hero's allies include a mentor, who may take any number of forms. The mentor may be a person (usually an older, wiser person, such as a teacher, parent, or friend), or it may be a deity or moral code (the hero's conscience, etc.) The mentor helps the hero but must not overcome his challenge for him.

Indy meets his mentor, Sallah, in Cairo. Sallah helps him navigate the Egyptian language and culture.

You've Got Mail is interesting in that Kathleen's mentor, NY152, and the villain, Joe Fox, are the same character.

Donkey is Shrek's mentor. He travels with Shrek, coaxes him toward Fiona, and asks him questions that force him to look within himself.

5   Approaching the dark moment

Your hero goes to confront the enemy, usually on the enemy's own turf.

Indy goes to the Nazi dig site.

Kathleen struggles to save her store.

Shrek journeys to the fiery keep of the dragon.

6   Dark moment

Here, your hero faces his biggest challenge, his most difficult battle. Test him to his limits before allowing him to triumph. Make it seem as though he must lose, as though there's no way out.

Indiana Jones finds the Ark of the Covenant in the

Well of Souls. Before he can climb out, however, his adversary, Belloq, takes the Ark and traps Indy and Marion inside the tomb. Dangerous snakes surrounded the two. As Belloq seals the only exit, Indy's torches begin to sputter and die. Hope is lost.

The crisis need not be a moment of physical peril for your hero, but it must seem as though the goal is lost. The Shop Around the Corner closes. There's nothing left to save. Kathleen is heartbroken.

When Shrek's goal shifts from recovering his swamp to being with Fiona, he decides to tell Fiona how he feels. He approaches her door and hears her say, "*Princess* and *ugly* don't go together. That's why I can't stay here with Shrek." This devastates him.

7 Return

The hero overcomes the dark moment, seizes the object of his quest, and begins the journey home, a hard road fraught with danger as the enemy tries to retake the prize.

In Indy's case, the enemy has already taken the prize. Indy must take it back, which he does a couple of times before the end of the story.

Kathleen learns to live without the store. Her boyfriend leaves. She takes up writing children's books as a new career, accepts a friendship offered by Joe Fox, and begins to rebuild her life. All the while, she continues to correspond with her on-line buddy, NY152.

Shrek obtains the deed to his swamp and returns home, yet he's not content.

8 Climax

The hero overcomes the final challenge in a second life-or-death struggle. It looks once more as though the villain must win.

The Nazis capture Indy and Marion, tie them to a

pillar, and open the Ark. The wrath of God pours out, killing everything in its path. Again, it appears there's no escape.

Kathleen discovers the kind of person Joe Fox really is, and she likes what she sees. Nevertheless, she can't forgive him for putting her bookstore out of business. Kathleen must choose between Joe Fox, a man for whom she has conflicted feelings, and NY152, the on-line crush she's never met.

Shrek learns of Fiona's feelings for him and races to take her back.

9   Permanence of the change

Just as your story must have a life-altering turning point for the hero, you must show that his change is permanent.

Indiana Jones changes little. He begins as a courageous treasure hunter and ends up much the same. One thing does change, however, and his life ultimately depends upon it. During the story's starting point, Army Intelligence questions him about the Ark. He knows the legend well but puts no stock in the alleged supernatural properties of the Ark itself.

At the end of the movie, he demonstrates his belief in the supernatural by telling Marion, rather emphatically, to close her eyes, to avoid looking at the Ark no matter what happens. His belief saves both their lives.

Kathleen finds out that NY152 *is* Joe Fox. When she says, "I wanted it to be you," we know she has changed. She lets go of her store, her former life, and any lingering resentment.

Throughout most of *Shrek*, Shrek just wants to be alone. In the end, he marries Fiona.

Look for these checkpoints in your plot. If any are missing, use the "suppose" method to develop ways to include them. Now you must get your characters from checkpoint to checkpoint in a way that keeps the reader engaged. To do this, maintain a high level of suspense.

Building Suspense

The following elements will increase the suspense in your story. Build as many into your plot as it can accommodate.

1   Make at least one character especially violent or adversarial.

    Early drafts of *Worlds Asunder* lacked an especially violent character who was frequently present in the story, so I added this trait to a character named Frank Lesperence. I'll discuss the specifics of Frank's evolution in the relevant sections throughout this book.

    In *Raiders of the Lost Ark*, an especially violent Nazi named Toht takes on several less-than-savory tasks.

    The nature and extent of violence in a story depends on its genre. In *You've Got Mail*, Joe Fox and his father aren't physically violent, yet both are ruthless in their approach to competitive business.

    In *Shrek*, Lord Farquaad doesn't do violence himself, but he orders it done on many occasions.

2   Spring surprises.

    Keep the reader guessing. Provide many obstacles that come at your hero when he least expects them and when your reader least expects them. Here are a few examples from the beginning of each movie:

Raiders of the Lost Ark
- In the opening scenes, both of Indy's colleagues betray him.
- Belloq takes the golden idol, establishing a behavior he'll repeat several times throughout the movie.

- Marion punches — not just slaps, but punches — Indy shortly after they meet in The Raven saloon.

You've Got Mail
- Kathleen's on-line buddy turns out to be the Big Bad Wolf, or in this case, the Big Bad Fox.
- Joe Fox feels bad about the things he said to Kathleen at the dinner party. He even helps her when she finds herself in the cash-only line at the supermarket with nothing but a credit card as payment.
- In the supermarket scene, at least, the Big Bad Fox turns out to be more charming than the sweet young hero.

Shrek
- Donkey's fairy dust wears off just when he thinks he'll escape Farquaad's men.
- Fairytale creatures fill Shrek's swamp as he sits down to a quiet dinner.
- Lord Farquaad changes the rules of the tournament. He declares that the knight who kills Shrek will be named Champion.

Notice that these surprises are not contrived events. They all stem from the characters, their goals, and their motivations. Provide at least one surprise turning point in each chapter of your book.

3   Mislead your reader.

Marion smiles when she first lays eyes on Indy. This makes the viewer believe Marion is happy to see him. Without this, it wouldn't surprise us when she punches him. Later, the viewer thinks Marion has died in a truck explosion — until she turns up alive at the Nazi dig site.

Joe Fox's behavior at the dinner party convinces us that he's nothing like the persona he presents as NY152, that he's really a rude, egotistical materialist who couldn't care less about the lives his business practices ruin. This sets up the surprise in the supermarket scene, where we learn he's not like that at all. "Mister Nasty" is a side of himself he struggles to control.

In *Shrek*, Dragon is set up as an obstacle to be overcome, and she is. The writers, however, let us assume she's male and evil. Both prove false.

If you mislead your reader, the surprises will have more impact. Nevertheless, you must play fair. Leave clues that are consistent with who your characters are — even if the characters are different than your reader believes them to be. Marion was pleased to see Indy only because his presence gave her a chance to confront him about their past. Joe Fox has some inner demons that stem from his tutelage by an uncaring capitalist father. Dragon was just protecting her home and her charge, Fiona.

4   Do your worst.

In every scene, ask yourself: What is the worst thing that could happen to the hero? Then make it happen.

George Lucas does this several times in the opening scene of *Raiders*. As Indy lifts the golden idol off its pedestal and replaces it with a bag of sand, the worst thing that can happen is for this to set off a series of deadly booby traps. As he tries to get away, the worst thing that can happen is for his partner to turn against him, escape with the idol, and leave Indy trapped inside. When Indy recovers the idol and escapes the temple despite the efforts of his traitorous partner, the worst thing that can happen is for someone more powerful to show up and claim the prize. All these things happen. The result is one of the most suspenseful scenes in the movie.

The worst thing that can happen to Joe Fox is for Kathleen Kelly to turn out to be his on-line crush, Shopgirl. The worst thing that can happen to Kathleen is for Fox Books to put her out of business. Both happen.

As Shrek and Donkey cross the rickety bridge over the boiling lake of lava, what's the worst thing that can happen? The bridge starts to fall apart, and Donkey, who's afraid of heights, refuses to go on? Would that be the worst? No, but it's a good start. The worst thing that could happen is for the bridge to collapse — someone, Dragon perhaps, incinerates it while the heroes are only halfway across. The former happens on the way into the castle, the latter on the way out.

When Shrek races to prevent Fiona's marriage to Lord Farquaad, the worst thing that can happen is for him to arrive late. The wedding is over. Fiona is already married. This happens. Fortunately, Dragon digests Farquaad, thereby invoking the until-death-do-us-part clause of Fiona's wedding vow.

5　Take away that which is most important to your hero.

What does your hero care about more than anything else? Take it away, or better yet, destroy it. At the very least, put it at risk.

Belloq does this repeatedly to Indiana Jones. First, he takes the golden idol, then Marion. Then he takes the Ark of the Covenant…twice.

The most important thing to Kathleen Kelly is her bookstore. Joe Fox destroys it.

When Shrek cares only about his swamp, Lord Farquaad takes it away. When Fiona supplants the swamp as Shrek's greatest desire, Farquaad returns the swamp and takes Fiona.

6　Haunt your hero with memories of a past failure.

Relate the failure to the events in the book. In *Worlds Asunder*, Chase recalls a horrible mistake he made during a previous investigation, a case involving the same pilot as the one in the case he must solve in the book.

When Belloq takes the golden idol at the beginning of

Raiders, he makes it clear that he's done this to Indy before. Indy's inability to hang on to his treasures plagues him throughout the movie.

Kathleen Kelly has failed to do anything she feels is significant. At one point she wonders whether this is because she likes the kind of life she has or whether it's because she lacks courage.

Shrek is haunted by the fact that nobody has ever loved him. He wants to tell Fiona how he feels, but he can't. Nobody could love an ogre, or so he believes.

7 Turn the environment loose upon your characters.

In *Worlds Asunder*, the vacuum of space lurks beyond the walls of the buildings, vehicles, and pressure suits that keep my characters alive. I frequently turn it loose inside.

For the purpose of building suspense, "environment" doesn't have to mean "natural phenomena." It can refer to any element of the character's surroundings that is beyond the control of the main characters, including sociological, political, or economic circumstances and events. Imagine your hero fleeing the Mafia. She can't go to the police because she's been framed for a crime she didn't commit. To complicate matters and build suspense, you might insert a political motorcade with all the necessary security forces, which she must avoid, to block her escape from a Mafia hit man. You can unleash the economy by making your hero lose her wallet. How will she do anything without money?

The temple Indy braves in the opening scene of the movie is an environment fraught with dangers. The desert extends from the Nazi dig site for three weeks in every direction, limiting Marion's escape possibilities and the means by which Indy can pursue the Ark. Snakes fill the Well of Souls. The power of the Ark presents yet another dangerous "environment" in the climactic scene.

Capitalism is unleashed in all its fury upon Kathleen Kelly and her little bookstore.

In *Shrek*, the lava is a force of nature that Dragon turns loose when she burns the bridge out from under the heroes.

8 Employ phobias.

What is your hero afraid of? Make him confront the source of his fear. If you choose something the reader also fears, it will heighten her emotional response.

"Snakes. Why did it have to be snakes?" This, perhaps the most remembered line from *Raiders of the Lost Ark*, stems from Indy's fear of snakes, a fear many viewers probably share.

Kathleen Kelly fears that she doesn't matter. She brings this up with her boyfriend early in the movie, and again in an email to NY152, in which she describes her life as "small." She's forced to face the reality of her smallness when her customers and other supporters abandon her and The Shop Around the Corner in favor of the big chain bookstore. Even her boyfriend leaves her.

In *Shrek*, the writers play on many people's fear of heights when Donkey becomes paralyzed on the castle's crumbling bridge. Shrek fears rejection. His fear almost costs him Fiona.

9 Never make anything easy.

The Nazis stay a step ahead of Indiana Jones. People constantly try to kill him. When Marion tries to drink Belloq under the table so she can escape, the drink turns out to be Belloq's family's label, which he's well accustomed to.

Kathleen's meek nature and lack of business savvy make her impossible battle against Fox Books even harder. All her efforts to save her business fail. Her new love interest, NY152, turns out to be the enemy. Nothing is easy.

Shrek finally decides to tell Fiona how he feels. He approaches her door and overhears part of a conversation in which Fiona says, "*Princess* and *ugly* don't go together. That's why I can't stay here with Shrek." This not only makes it harder for Shrek to talk to her, it makes it impossible.

10 Show that the danger is real.

Hurt your hero, kill a good guy, or both. If you kill someone your hero cares about, it will raise the personal stakes and inject a strong emotional element into your plot. At one point in *Worlds Asunder*, Chase is hospitalized for his wounds following a battle for his life. In addition, several good guys die, including one of Chase's closest relatives.

During the opening scenes of the movie, both of Indy's traitorous companions die, one in the temple, the other at the hands of Belloq. We know from the outset that Indy's enemies and the archeological sites themselves are dangerous.

The dangers don't have to be physical. Joe Fox announces to his father, the patriarch of Fox Books, that one independent bookstore has already gone out of business. This demonstrates the danger to The Shop Around the Corner.

When Fiona says she can't stay with Shrek because *princess* and *ugly* don't go together, it hurts Shrek deeply.

11 Impose a deadline.

This is the ticking clock. It need not be a clock the hero can see, or one with a specified time to zero, but one way or another you must create a sense of urgency.

In *Worlds Asunder*, the political events surrounding Chase's investigation escalate toward war. If he can solve the case in time, his findings might diffuse the building crisis. He doesn't know how much time he has, but he and the reader can see the escalation. In alternating scenes, Chase takes a step toward solving the case, and then political events expand. This creates an unseen clock. Chase and the reader are never quite sure it hasn't already reached zero, the point beyond which no one can stop the war.

Indiana Jones must find the Ark before the Nazis do.

Kathleen Kelly must save The Shop Around the Corner before she runs out of money.

Shrek must get to Princess Fiona before she marries Lord Farquaad.

12 Prevent your hero from running away.

You don't need to impose a physical barrier, but make your hero's need to stay in the conflict stronger than his desire to escape it. The same must be true for your villain.

In *Worlds Asunder,* Chase wants to retire and go home to his family — that would be his escape — but averting war is much more important. He won't quit, even when the stakes rise and he must risk losing his daughter.

The Ark of the Covenant must not fall into Nazi hands. The magnitude of the consequences keeps Indy in the conflict, even after he loses the Ark to them twice.

The Shop Around the Corner is all Kathleen has. In her mind, it defines her. She must fight to save it.

When it comes down to it, Shrek's love for Fiona far outweighs his desire to live alone.

13 Include a final twist near the end.

Your ending must have two important characteristics: It must surprise the reader and it must seem inevitable. These requirements are not contradictory.

There are two twists near the end of *Raiders*. First, Indy decides to give the Ark to the Nazis rather than destroy it. Second, the power of the Ark consumes those who open it. Both are surprising. Indiana Jones has been risking his life throughout the movie to keep the Ark out of Nazi hands, and we have seen little or no evidence of anything supernatural.

In retrospect, however, both events are inevitable. Indy has devoted his life to the preservation of ancient artifacts. He can't bring himself to destroy this one. As for the power of the Ark, the writers have touted this alleged power too often to make the Ark ultimately impotent.

When Kathleen Kelly learns that Joe Fox is NY152, it surprises her. Yet the viewer has known all along. The twist for the viewer is that Kathleen is actually happy about it. She *wants* to be with the enemy. Yet this is inevitable. Kathleen should be happy. Now she doesn't have to choose.

In *Shrek*, Princess Fiona is afflicted by a curse in which she's an ogre at night and a beautiful woman during the day. Because this is a fairytale, the viewer expects a happy ending; he expects Fiona to break the curse and become the beautiful princess 24/7. She doesn't. She becomes the ogre. This surprises the viewer because it's not what he expected. Yet upon reflection, it's inevitable. Shrek and Fiona have fallen in love, so the ending will be happy only if they end up together. Throughout the story, we see hints that Fiona would enjoy an ogre's lifestyle (fighting bandits on the road, singing sweetly to a bird and then making its head explode, blowing up frogs and snakes into balloons, etc.). Shrek, on the other hand, could never be content as a prince, with all the expectations and scrutiny that come with public life. He'd be miserable. Therefore, when Fiona breaks the curse, she must become the ogre.

14   Use these techniques in combination.

The Well of Souls represents a combination of suspense builders. Snakes, a danger of the environment, force Indy to confront his phobia. He's haunted by his past failures when Belloq claims the Ark, the thing most important to Indy. Finally, losing the Ark and being sealed in the tomb with the snakes are the two worst things that can happen. These culminate in Indy's dark moment.

Look for all these elements in your plot. If any are missing use the "suppose" method to generate ideas to eliminate the deficiencies.

Character Arc

If your plot is character-driven, as it should be, you know how your characters affect your plot. You must also understand how your plot affects your characters. To do this, make a character arc table, like the example for *Shrek* shown in Figure 2.

In the first row, list the main characters (the hero, the villain, and any prominent supporting characters). Use the second row to describe the starting point of each character's arc, the aspect of the character that will change during the story. Write the major plot events in the left-hand column. For this purpose, consider any event that nudges a character along her arc to be a major plot event. These may or may not be the checkpoints in the mythic structure. In each column, describe how each event affects each character.

Not every event will affect every character in a way that will push her along her arc, as illustrated by the numerous blank cells in the table. Furthermore, you may have some supporting characters who don't change. That's okay. People learn and grow from their experiences, however, and having these characters evolve in some way will help make them multi-dimensional.

Keep your character arc table handy as you write or revise your scenes. Refer to it often. Doing so will help you keep track of the mindset of your characters. It will remind you to make each character's change appropriately evident as events unfold.

Major Plot Events	Shrek	Fiona	Lord Farquaad
Initial state	Shrek doesn't like people. He just wants to live alone.	Fiona is trapped in a castle and cursed. She dreams of being rescued by her Prince Charming.	Farquaad believes that he is a king. He wants only to clear the fairytale creatures from his kingdom.
A horde of fairytale creatures shows up at Shrek's swamp.	Shrek is forced to interact with others: first Donkey, then Farquaad, and finally Fiona.		
Farquaad learns that he's not technically a king and that he must marry a princess to become a king.			Farquaad is no longer content. He feels he must become a king.
Farquaad sends Shrek to rescue Fiona.	This puts Shrek on a collision course with the future love of his life.		
Shrek rescues Fiona from the fiery keep of the dragon.	Shrek meets the future love of his life.	Fiona is disappointed to learn that her rescuer is an ogre. She plans to marry Lord Farquaad to break her curse.	
Shrek and Fiona walk the long road back to Lord Farquaad.	Shrek learns that he has much in common with Fiona. He falls in love with her.	Fiona learns that she has much in common with Shrek. She falls in love with him.	
Donkey has a starlight conversation with Shrek.	Donkey makes Shrek realize that his problem might not be with other people; it might be within himself.		

Figure 2. Character arc table
continued over

Major Plot Events	Shrek	Fiona	Lord Farquaad
A conversation takes place between Donkey and Fiona inside the windmill.	Shrek overhears part of the conversation and misunderstands Fiona. Heartbroken, he goes off to fetch Lord Farquaad.	Fiona realizes that she could be happy with Shrek.	
Shrek returns home and Fiona goes with Farquaad.	Shrek realizes that he will no longer be happy alone.	Fiona realizes that she could not be happy with Lord Farquaad.	Farquaad marries Fiona and becomes a real king, though only briefly.
Shrek learns of Fiona's feelings for him.	Shrek feels a renewed sense of hope and races to get Fiona back.		
Shrek rescues Fiona from Lord Farquaad and marries her.	Shrek's change is permanent. He will no longer live alone.	Fiona's change is permanent. She has chosen Shrek over any Prince Charming. Her curse is broken.	Farquaad's need to be a true king has cost him his life. That too is permanent.

Figure 2. Character arc table

Exercises

1   Watch one of your favorite movies. Look for the nine checkpoints in the mythic structure. Can you find them? Note how far into the story each occurs. Repeat this for several movies. You'll begin to see the variety of ways in which these checkpoints can be applied.

2   Review your own plot outline (or read your manuscript). Does your plot have all nine checkpoints? If not, for each missing checkpoint, think of three story changes that would allow you to include it. Consider how these changes will affect your hero and your plot, decide which idea will work best in your story, and make the changes necessary to incorporate the idea.

3   Review your plot outline (or read your manuscript). Look for each suspense builder listed in this chapter. Have you used them all? If not, for each missing element, think of three story changes that would allow you to include it. Consider how these changes will affect the level of suspense, decide which idea will work best in your story, and make the changes necessary to incorporate the idea.

4   Make a character arc table. Do your hero, your villain, and *all* of your prominent supporting characters go through a change, no matter how small or subtle, as a result of the events in the story? If not, for each static character, consider what change he might go through. Note the change on your character arc table. Make the change evident as you write or rewrite your scenes.

4

First Draft

Some people would say a chapter on writing the first draft has no place in a book about revision. I would not dispute such an argument. Nevertheless, I include it here for those who've done what I did when I wrote *Worlds Asunder*: written their first draft without putting enough thought into the topics of the previous chapters. For these folks, this chapter isn't about the first draft. It's about the first revision (or the fifth, twelfth, or twentieth). Your prose may be so polished it sparkles, but if you haven't properly considered your setting, characters, and plot, your book won't sell.

As you write, or rewrite, your work of fiction (be it a short story or novel), you'll write it in scenes. This chapter includes some fundamental tips for getting these scenes onto paper. Don't worry about the quality of your scenes; you'll take care of that in Chapter 9. For now, you just need a scene break anytime you change the viewpoint character, abruptly change locations, or have a jump in time.

Point of View

Every scene must be shown from the viewpoint of one of your characters. In general, if your hero is in the scene, show the events from her point of view. The more you show from her viewpoint, the better your reader will get to know her and the more your reader will care about what happens to her. Furthermore, if you're writing from a single viewpoint or in first person, you must stick with that single viewpoint. Otherwise, choose another viewpoint character when one or more of the following statements are true:

1   Your hero isn't in the scene.

2   Another character is in the hot seat. Show the scene from the viewpoint of the character who has the most to lose if events go badly. This character should usually be your hero.

3   You must convey some overwhelmingly important piece of information your hero doesn't know.

Use these opportunities to show how other characters feel about your hero.

Setting

Each scene will take place somewhere. In other words, each scene will have a setting. And each setting will include elements that affect every human sense: sight, hearing, smell, touch, and taste. You must write it as such.

Before you do, make an index card, like those shown in Figures 3 and 4, upon which you can write the setting's description. This setting card will become a handy reference that will help you keep the setting consistent throughout your novel.

Ask yourself: What impression do I want to make? That the place is desolate? Opulent? Filthy? Dangerous? Foreign? Something more subtle? Whatever the impression, write it on the card first. Then describe the setting as experienced by each of the five senses. Select a few details that will promote the impression you want to make. Work these details into the action of the scene.

Find ways to use elements of your setting to affect your characters and plot. I'm not talking about having your character sit on the beanbag chair, lean on the granite countertop, or walk across the plush, forest-green carpet. I'm talking about using the fountain pen on the desk as a murder weapon, encoding a message that your hero must decipher into the wall tapestry, or shooting a hole through a window that looks out upon the vast vacuum of space while your characters are standing nearby. These elements will force your characters to interact with their setting. It will make the setting an integral part of your story.

If the setting has changed substantially since the last time the reader saw it (a bomb has gone off in the room, a murder has taken place there, etc.), create a new setting card.

Create a new card if you want to use an old setting to create a new impression. Provide a reason for the change of impression. You don't want to confuse the reader about what the place is like or make the character experiencing it seem inconsistent.

Figures 3 and 4 show a pair of setting cards from *Worlds Asunder*. The setting has changed little between these two scenes and in each scene it will be described as seen through the eyes of the same viewpoint character. The circumstances, however, are different, as are the impressions I want to make. Notice how the desired impression determines which details I choose to present.

SETTING: Cockpit of the *Phoenix* as it was found at the crash site

IMPRESSION: Sinister, grave-like.

DESCRIPTION: Unsecured items litter the floor. Padded seats hang from the ceiling like stalactites. Displays are dark.

SIGHTS: Agent Lederman lies face-up, his helmet removed. The moisture has leached out of his body, leaving a desiccated husk behind.

SOUNDS: Voices of the evidence-recovery teams marking the location of the debris outside.

SMELLS: Fresh, life-sustaining air in Chase's pressure suit.

FEELINGS: Oppressive heat (110C in the lunar sun). Low-g of lunar gravity.

TASTE: Same as smell.

HOW THE SETTING AFFECTS THE PLOT: Clues provide a means for Chase to solve the case, if he can collect them before the onset of lunar night.

HOW THE SETTING AFFECTS THE CHARACTERS: Clues initially suggest pilot error, a conclusion that Chase hopes to avoid.

Figure 3. Setting card for the Phoenix *cockpit (at the crash site)*

SETTING: Cockpit of the *Phoenix* during the re-enactment of the crash

IMPRESSION: Made-up, simulator-like.

DESCRIPTION: The cockpit is rotated 135 degrees from right-side up (the way it was found at the crash site). Clues are arrayed as they were found at the site. An EVA suit near the door represents Lederman's body.

SIGHTS: Muted gray interior; electronics consoles are dark, durapane windshield is undamaged. Corrugated hanger door beyond the window.

SOUNDS: Voices of the technicians and the hum of data analysis equipment emanates from the cargo compartment.

SMELLS: Stale oxygen and sweat resulting from poor circulation of hanger bay air into the cockpit.

FEELINGS: Warm and crowded. Movements awkward because of cockpit orientation. Low-g of lunar gravity.

TASTE: Same as smell

HOW THE SETTING AFFECTS THE PLOT: The complexity of the clues and the results of the reenactment drive Snider's anxiety higher and force a confrontation between him and Chase that puts Snider on the suspect list.

HOW THE SETTING AFFECTS THE CHARACTERS: The physical clues and information from the analysts drive the dialogue and Chase's conclusions. Chase's ability to clear Randy of wrongdoing or negligence rides on the evidence scattered about him.

Figure 4. Setting card for the Phoenix *cockpit (in the hangar bay)*

You also might change the reader's impression of a setting when you describe it from a different character's viewpoint. A poor man might walk into a middle-class home and find it opulent. A millionaire might look upon the same house with disdain. Use the details the character notices, and the thoughts those details evoke, as ways to portray the characters as distinct individuals.

Choosing the right details can influence how your reader perceives your setting. Picking those details now will help you build them into your scene as you write. You may also find it helpful to sketch the setting on the back of the card. Review the card before you write another scene that takes place in the same setting. Doing so will help you keep the details consistent.

Write the First Draft

If you've already written your first draft, go through the steps discussed in the previous chapters (and in the first two sections of this chapter) and consider this a rewrite step. The rewrite may be so extensive that you'll feel like you're writing a first draft. In *Worlds Asunder,* I threw away the first five chapters and rewrote them, as seven new chapters, from scratch. Many scenes throughout the book received this same treatment. If this is what your manuscript needs, do it. The result will be well worth the effort.

Writing the first draft is the most difficult step for many writers. They can't find the time; they read the passage they've just written and decide it needs work, so they go back to edit; or they don't know what to write next or how to write it. Having a good knowledge of your characters and an outline of your plot will go a long way toward solving the latter problem, but it's often not enough.

Writing the first draft is a right-brain (creative brain) process. The vast majority of the problems writers experience during first draft are due to inappropriate left-brain (analytical brain) interference.[1] The left brain says things like:

- "This scene stinks. I need to go back and fix it."
- "Nobody's ever going to read this."
- "I need to think this through before I write it."
- "I don't know this subject very well. I'd better do more research before I write."
- "I really need to do the grocery shopping, the laundry, or the dishes."
- "I just don't have time to write."

With this kind of talk in your head, it's no wonder you can't get words onto the page. You need to silence your analytical brain, your editor. Shut it up long enough for your creative brain, your muse, to write. Here are some things you can do to trick your editor into submission:

1   Get up early.

Your editor sleeps when you do. Your muse dreams all night.[1] If you get up early in the morning, you can write for a couple of hours before your editor wakes up. Skip the coffee, however. Your editor needs the caffeine. Your muse doesn't.

2   Separate yourself from distractions.

I write my first drafts between the hours of 4:00 and 6:00 in the morning, before I go to my day job. My wife and five-year-old son are still asleep, the television and radio are off, the phone doesn't ring. The house is quiet. It's ideal.

I usually get 1000 to 1500 words a day onto paper this way. I can write a novel in three months. I wrote the first draft of this book in just nineteen days.

3   Write by hand.

I know what you're thinking. *In this day and age, I'm supposed to write by hand? You can't be serious.* I am. Typing is a left-brain process. Writing longhand, particularly in cursive, is a right-brain process. Writing by hand helps keep your editor dormant. Though some writers consider this an extra step, others have been surprised by how much it helps. Try writing a couple of scenes by hand with a good-quality pen, one that fits comfortably in your hand and writes so smoothly that it won't slow you down. Use large sheets of unlined paper. Your editor likes lines and boundaries, your muse doesn't.[1]

Personally, I've found it unnecessary to write by hand to keep my editor dormant, though I still do it frequently when I'm away from my computer. Instead, I close my eyes as I type — there go the lines and boundaries that my editor likes so much. This practice also keeps me from seeing misspelled words that would otherwise prompt me to correct my typos, which would wake up my editor and shut down the flow of creativity that I need to compose my first draft.

4   Don't stop to edit.

Don't sweat the quality of your first draft. It's a rare author who gets it right the first time. Whatever weaknesses appear in your style; whatever inconsistencies plague your characters and plot; however badly your scenes or manuscript may be organized; no matter how poor your grammar, spelling, and punctuation are — whatever mistakes you make — correct them later. That's what revision is for. If you get bogged down in editing now, you may spend weeks polishing a scene that you'll eventually have to throw away. Don't waste the time. Get your story onto paper now. Polish what you keep later.

If you have an idea that contradicts something you've already written, make a note in the margin (if you're typing, put the note in brackets) and continue writing as if you've already resolved the inconsistency. You've made a note on the manuscript. You won't forget to make the corrections later. Just keep writing.

If you can't think of a word you need, leave a blank or write down a similar word that does come to mind. Make a note to find the right word later. Don't wake up your editor with a search through the nearest thesaurus. In my experience, the word I'm looking for is too different from the one I wrote down to find in a thesaurus anyway.

5 Don't stop to research.

Let's say you need to describe Barcelona in the springtime, but you've never been there. Don't run to the Internet for pictures. Just make a note: "What does Barcelona look like in the spring?" Then keep writing. If you need to find out how a forklift works, write: "How does a forklift work?" You'll have time later to fill in the missing details. Don't arrest your muse during the first draft with a digression into research.

Scene Cards

When I'm in the throes of writing the first draft, I don't stop for anything. If I get halfway though a sentence and decide it's not what I want to write, I start the sentence I want without going back to delete the remnants of the old. I'm not suggesting you go that far, but it illustrates how determined I am to keep my editor silent. When I'm finished creating for the day, however, I go back and write a scene card for each new scene.[2]

What is a scene card? First and foremost, it's a timesaving tool, a handy record of information you'll need later. When you get into revision, having some basic facts on an index card will save you hours of sifting through your scenes to find the information you need.

Specifically, jot down the following:

1   Scene name

This name will never appear in the book. It's just to remind you which scene the card is for. It will help you identify your scenes quickly when you start organizing them within your manuscript.

2   Scene number

Number the cards in the order in which the scenes appear in your first draft, just in case you accidentally drop them. Renumber the cards if you change the order of your scenes later.

3   Scene type

Is the scene an action scene? A romance scene? A dialogue scene? Something else? Write it on the card. This information will become important when you examine the order of your scenes. You don't want too many of the same kind of scene in a row.

4   Viewpoint character

You'll use this when you evaluate character consistency and when you look back at your characters' arcs.

5   Names of the characters in the scene

Make this a quick list; you don't need full names. These names will help when you look at characterization within your scenes.

6 Setting

Just write the name of the place, like "Armstrong Lounge" or "Lunar Alpha Control Room." Later, you'll look at where each scene takes place and ask: Can I achieve a better effect by moving this scene to a different location?

7 The conflict

If your scene includes conflict, describe it in a few words. Later, you'll evaluate each scene specifically for conflict and tension.

8 Points that advance the plot

If your scene advances the plot in some way, note how. Every scene should advance the plot, reveal character, or both. You'll ensure later that every scene does. For now, if the scene doesn't, just write, "None."

9 Points that reveal character

If you've revealed something about a character, introduced a new character, provided important character-background information, developed a relationship between characters, or pushed a character along her arc, note it.

10 Inconsistencies

If you wrote anything in the scene that you know conflicts with an earlier scene, note the inconsistency.

11 Other important information

Note any information in the scene that's important for the reader to know, such as technical descriptions, important bits of history, etc. If you delete the scene later, this will tell you what information you may need to incorporate elsewhere in your manuscript.

12 Research questions

If any research questions came up during the first-draft phase ("How does a forklift work?"), note them. I'll discuss research in Chapter 5.

13 Suspense elements introduced

These are questions you've raised in the reader's mind, any loose ends you need to tie up. Later, you'll make sure you've resolved them all.

14 Suspense elements resolved

If you resolved suspense elements introduced in earlier scenes, note them.

An example scene card from *Worlds Asunder* is shown in Figure 5. Continue this process, scene by scene, until your whole manuscript is on paper, beginning to end. If you wrote your first draft by hand, type it into your computer.

NO. 3

SCENE: Control Tower — *Phoenix* Hits the Ground

TYPE: Action/Suspense

VIEWPOINT: Snider

CHARACTERS: Snider, Brower, Chavez, Robinson, Others

SETTING: Control tower, Lunar Alpha Base

CONFLICT: Snider vs. time and circumstances — trying to prevent the *Phoenix* from crashing

PLOT POINTS: *Phoenix* crashes. Emergency Response Team deployed

CHAR POINTS: Introduction of Brower. More of Snider's personality — how he handles a crisis.

INCONSISTENCIES: None

OTHER INFO: Some background on the workings of NASA

RESEARCH TOPICS: How is mission control currently handled at NASA (extrapolate to future setting)?

SUSP ELEMENTS: Will the occupants of the *Phoenix* survive?

SUSP RESOLVED: None

Figure 5. Scene card

Exercises

1   Pick a scene from a work of fiction you've written. Make sure the scene has multiple characters, contains conflict, and that at least one character has something to lose if events don't go his way. Based on the guidelines in this chapter, have you chosen the best viewpoint character? If not, decide which character has the most to lose and rewrite the scene from that character's viewpoint. Don't just change a few references. Change your wording throughout the scene to convey the thoughts, attitude, and emotional state of the viewpoint character.

Write the scene again, this time from the viewpoint of a character who has little or nothing at stake. Change your wording to convey this character's thoughts, attitude, and emotional state. How does this affect the level of tension in the scene? Have someone read both versions. Ask the reader which she liked better and why.

2   Make a setting card for the scene in Exercise 1. Include all five senses in your description. Find a way to make the setting affect your characters, plot, or both. Rewrite the scene to include every element on your setting card without stopping the action. Have someone read both versions of the scene. Ask the reader which she liked better and why.

3   Write a scene by hand using a good-quality pen on unlined paper (printer paper will do). Don't stop to consider word choice. Don't stop to edit. If you need to research a topic, just note the question to be answered in the margin and keep writing. Don't stop for anything until the scene is on paper, beginning to end. Did it take more or less time than it would have taken you to write a scene of similar length and complexity on the

computer? Did the scene go down smoothly or were you troubled by writer's block?

4   Make a scene card for the scene from Exercise 3. If you come back to this scene a month from now, how much easier will it be to find this information on the card than it would be to search for it, scene by scene, through your manuscript?

Part II

The Big Stuff

Now that you've gotten your manuscript onto paper, what do you do with it? Looking back, it's about as rough as a draft can be. It's disorganized, your characters are shoddy and often without emotion, your plot is rife with inconsistencies, you have gaping holes in your research, your dialogue sounds phony, your prose contains every style weakness known to humankind, and you haven't got a clue how the thing is supposed to be formatted.

Have no fear. That's what revision is for.

5

Research

In Chapter 1, I said you need to get the details of the culture, technology, and setting correct but that you don't have to do all of the research up front. Instead, do only the bare minimum required to develop your basic story line and characters before you write the first draft.

As you write, note the topics you need to research — the specific questions you need to answer. This practice will limit your research to that which you actually need for your story. Otherwise, you may spend months or years researching facts that you'll never need.

Before I wrote *Worlds Asunder*, I knew I wanted to base the story on the Moon, which I knew very little about. I purchased a technical guide to our solar system and read the single, ten-page chapter that discussed the Moon. This chapter gave me such facts as the natural resources that can be found there — resources that my characters might be willing to suffer conflict over. How's that for having a setting that will affect the plot? The ten-page chapter also provided the basics of lunar geology and geography, the length of the lunar day and night, and the force of lunar gravity — enough to decide what types of characters to put there and to build a story around them.

Similarly, if you're not familiar with your main character's profession, you may need to discuss it with an expert in the field. If your hero's a cop, you might arrange a ride-along with your local police department and discuss practices and procedures with an officer. Don't spend months on this. Get the basics. Get a feel for the nature of the job. Save the details for later.

After I wrote the first draft of *Worlds Asunder*, I knew what additional lunar details I needed, such as daytime and nighttime temperatures, the amount of time it takes to orbit the Moon at a given distance from its surface, and the names of some of the less-prominent craters and features. I researched only the answers to my specific questions.

This approach saved me months, or years, spent learning everything I'll never need to know about the Moon.

At this point, I also researched all the other little things that came up during my first draft, like how a space suit works, the acceleration force induced by a space shuttle launch from Earth, the organizational structure of the CIA, and the symptoms of cyanide poisoning.

Go through your scene cards and consolidate your list of research questions. Then track down the answers. Start with the Internet for the miscellaneous questions. Check out books from the library, if you need to, or talk to experts in the field. For your hero cop, go back to the police department and get your detailed questions answered.

Compile the research in a convenient place, and then go back to your manuscript and fill in the blanks.

Exercises

1 Consider a scene you haven't already written that requires some technical details on a topic with which you're only causally familiar. Research the topic before you write the scene. Gather all the information you might need, any little detail that might come in handy. Then write the scene. Did you use every detail you gathered during your research? If not, how much time might you have saved by researching only the things you needed?

puppet scene
(Bad)

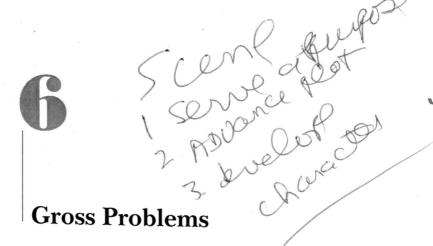

6

Gross Problems

In this chapter, you'll apply field dressings to the gaping wounds in your manuscript. To do this, work primarily from your scene cards rather than from the manuscript itself. Take notes on the backs of the cards as you work through the sections below.

Scene Purpose

Each scene must serve a purpose. It must advance the plot or develop character, preferably both. If it does these things, you should have noted it on your scene card. A scene that does neither is a digression or it just conveys information. Delete the scene and find another way to provide any necessary information. Make a note on the card of any scene you plan to move information to.

Your scene should also show conflict between characters, create suspense, and show how the day-to-day life in your world is different from your reader's life. Jot down ideas to enhance these characteristics of your scene.

Puppet Scenes

A puppet scene is a conversation whose sole purpose is to convey information to the reader.

Consider this example from a critique submission in which a boy named Antonio has woken up in the middle of the night with his legs tangled in sugarcane:

> Maria hugged her doll and rolled over in her sleep. Her bright red dress twisted around her legs as she moved.
> "I guess I got all twisted up, too." Antonio smiled down at her and sighed. "I wish I were only three again, Maria ..."

Here, Antonio is talking to his sleeping sister. The passage provides some good characterization. It shows that Antonio cares for Maria and that he longs for a simpler time. But look at what he says next:

> "... Mamá would still be alive and I could hug her. I could play with my friends back in México and even go to the convent school where the teachers made learning English fun. But now, we're hidden in a sugarcane field to save our lives. When we ran from the Federales, Mamá got sick and died and Papá had to leave us here while he went to seek help."

Here, Antonio's no longer talking to Maria. He's talking to the reader, and he's doing so only to provide backstory. 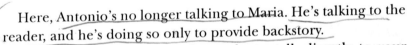 Never use your characters' mouths to talk directly to your reader. In this example, the problem merely encompasses a small passage, a dialogue problem that I'll discuss in more detail in Chapter 12. For now, if you find an entire scene of informative dialogue, cut the scene and find another way to convey the information.

Static Conversations

A static conversation contains dialogue without much action or conflict.

Suppose two characters sit at the kitchen table conversing over a cup of tea. The discussion may be interesting. It may even contain verbal conflict and tension. But if the characters are just talking, they'll probably bore your reader. Get your characters out of the kitchen, put them someplace interesting, and give them something to do while they talk.

If one of your characters likes to work in her garden, move the conversation to the front yard and have her tend her plants while she talks. Doing so will reinforce this aspect of her character. *Suppose* snails have eaten her strawberry plants down to the stems. This will add tension because she'll already be upset when her friend starts the conversation the scene is really about.

If one of your characters wants to keep the discussion secret, put the nosy next-door neighbor in his yard; maybe he'll overhear. One character wants to postpone the conversation, but the other won't shut up. Now you have three levels of tension: the dialogue, the snail problem, and the neighbor. How much more interesting will this scene be than if it had taken place at the kitchen table?

For each static conversation, find ways to improve the scene and note your ideas on the back of the scene card.

Organization

Don't string too many action scenes in a row. You want to excite your reader, not fatigue him. Similarly, don't put several passive scenes together; you'll risk boring the reader.

I color-code the top row of my scene cards with highlighter markers (pink for action scenes, yellow for passive, orange for others) and lay the cards out on a table with the top row showing. This gives me a good visual display of the distribution of action. Then I look for scenes that I can move to create a better balance.

In the "Building Suspense" section of Chapter 3, I mentioned that *Worlds Asunder* lacked an especially violent character, so I added this trait to a minor character named Frank Lesperence. I composed a violent confrontation between him and my hero. During this organization step, I decided where to insert the new scene. Because it was a tense scene, I put it in the middle of a series of relatively passive scenes. Doing so not only helped balance the action in the book but made a minor character more interesting, gave the hero an additional suspect, gave the villain an additional tool, and ultimately increased the suspense in the story.

As a counterexample, I had a scene in which Bill Ryan, one of the good guys, recovers from a coma with his romantic interest at his bedside. It didn't matter where I put the scene, as long as it occurred near the end of the story — I didn't want to give away too early that the man would live.

I reviewed the last several scenes of the book. As Chase's story approached its climax, I found a single action scene that was half again as long as most of my chapters, at a time when chapters should be getting shorter. So I chose a point of high tension in the scene, added one sentence to create a cliffhanger, and ended the chapter. I opened the next chapter with a jump cut to the passive coma-recovery scene before returning to the action. The result: better balance of the action, shorter chapters near the end of the book to promote the illusion of a quickening pace, and greater suspense.

Checking Your Characters' Arcs

Each scene in which a character takes a step along her arc should have a note describing that step on the scene card. Go through your cards and list these changes, by character, on a separate sheet of paper. Now compare the list with your character arc table. Have your characters progressed in the manner you intended? Are your character's changes appropriately evident in each scene? If not, note on the back of the scene card any revisions you'll need to make.

Resolving Inconsistencies

As you wrote your first draft you may have made decisions that created inconsistencies in your characters or plot. If so, decide how best to resolve them, and in which scenes. Note any necessary changes on the backs of the scene cards.

Resolving Suspense Elements

You should have noted on your scene cards the suspense elements you introduced or resolved in each scene. Go through the cards now. On a separate sheet of paper, list each suspense element. Next to it, write down the number of the scene in which you introduced it and the number of the scene in which you resolved it.

Did you resolve them all? If not, tie up each loose end. Either find a scene in which to resolve it or don't bring it up in the first place. Make notes on the appropriate scene cards.

In *Worlds Asunder*, I leave only one unresolved suspense element, which I introduced about halfway through the book. In this case, I violated one of my own guidelines, but I did so to achieve a specific effect. In the epilogue, I remind the reader that it remains unresolved and hint that it will spark a new conflict. This hook, I hope, will lure my readers into buying the sequel, *Venus Rain*.

The Opening

Now set aside your scene cards, pick up your manuscript, and read the first chapter.

Make it clear from the outset who your hero is. Write the first scene of Chapter 1 from your hero's point of view. I go a step further and make my hero the first named character in the book. Your reader will pick up on these cues. If you start Chapter 1 from the viewpoint of some other character, your reader will incorrectly assume that this character is the hero, which might cause confusion later on.

Many people will read the first page of a book while they're standing in the bookstore deciding which book to buy.[1] If your story doesn't rev up by the bottom of the first page, you'll probably lose these readers. Therefore, give your hero an immediate desire, even if it's just a cup of coffee, and place an obstacle between him and the thing he wants. Otherwise your opening will lack tension.

Worlds Asunder begins:

"It was really embarrassing." Edward "Chase" Morgan drew the top card from the deck: the queen of diamonds. "We'd just returned from hitting a crack factory and warehouse in Cuba. This was back when President Montros thought he could stop the drug trade with air strikes."

He tapped his cards on the table. Michelle Fairchild, his materials engineering intern from Mars Tech, had won every game that evening. Not this one, though, if he could help it. Chase needed just two cards to win and Michelle hadn't lain down any of hers. Unfortunately, the queen wasn't one of the two. He tossed it onto the discard pile.

Smiling, Michelle picked it up, then placed it and two others on the table.

Chase groaned. That group put her in the lead and, at double or nothing, the credits were starting to add up.

The opening dialogue promises an embarrassing story about my hero, Chase Morgan. It hooks the reader in just four words. The rest of the paragraph reveals Chase as an adventurous character, the card game gives him an immediate want, Michelle presents an obstacle to victory, and the credits provide the stakes of the game.

As the scene progresses, I show Chase caring (in a paternal manner) for both his intern and his dog, poking fun at himself, and losing the game graciously. The scene gives the reader several reasons to like him.

Because you need to show a snippet of your hero's normal life before crisis disrupts it, you might not introduce the external conflict (your hero's goal in the story) until some time later. Nevertheless, reveal his goal before the end of the first chapter. In *Worlds Asunder*, I do this about two pages later:

The comm panel buzzed. Chase stretched his lanky frame and got to his feet, then leapt to the terminal against the slight lunar g.

He keyed the link. On the screen, a frown elongated the narrow face of Security Chief Stan Brower, whose sharp eyes were nearly as pale as his graying hair. This wouldn't be good news.

"We've got a ship in trouble," Brower said. "The *Phoenix*. Snider needs you to assemble a team..."

> [Chase] logged into NASA's data net and scanned the
> *Phoenix* file. A freighter, the record said. Local, its opera-
> tions restricted to lunar destinations. Good. That limited
> the crew size and fuel reserves on board. He scrolled past
> the physical statistics — size, class, thrust-to-mass ratio
> — and came to the corporate data.
>   OWNER: Stellarfare
>   CREW: Randy Lauback, Phyllis Conway
>   He read the last line again. His investigations career
> had come full circle, it seemed. It would end where it had
> begun. With Randy Lauback.
>   **Chase knew then that he had to take the case, how-
> ever long it might last, and follow it through to com-
> pletion. He owed Randy that much.**

This not only defines his goal, solving the *Phoenix* case, but also gives him a personal stake (some unspecified, yet important, history involving the ship's pilot).

If you haven't accomplished these things in Chapter 1, find ways to do so. This may mean deleting scenes from the beginning of your book and starting the story when the crisis occurs; it may mean changing the viewpoint character of the opening scene or moving a different scene — one written from the hero's view-point — to the front of the book; or it may mean accelerating the pace by moving background information to later pages.

Take notes on the scene cards of any affected scenes.

Enhancing Setting

Read through each scene of your manuscript three times. During the first reading, find opportunities to show how the day-to-day life of your characters differs from that of your reader, who wants your story to carry him away from his mundane world. Bring out the set-ting elements that are specific to your setting's time period, coun-try, or culture. If your story takes place in the present day, show setting elements that are specific to your character or her situation. If she's a cop, show her cleaning her gun or escorting handcuffed prisoners through the police station. Make her sweat in her Kevlar vest. Include the sounds of sirens and the clanging of iron doors, and have her say something only a police officer would say. Now the reader has a sense of what your character's world is like.

Consider this excerpt from the opening scene of *Worlds Asunder*:

> Chase sucked the last of the coffee from his **seal-pak mug,** then checked the date for probably the fifth time that day. Just two more weeks to retirement. Then he could go **home to Earth** and what was left of his family.

In this paragraph, Chase holds not just a mug, but a seal-pak mug. The reader doesn't know exactly what this is, but with a reference to the slight lunar gravity a few sentences later, she can fill in the blanks. The reader also knows from this paragraph that Chase is not on Earth, which certainly makes his setting different than the reader's here and now.

Consider the following passage, from which I've stripped the portions that set Chase's world apart from that of the reader:

> "Morgan to tower."
>
> "Tower. Go ahead Morgan."
>
> "Tell me about the *Phoenix*."
>
> "Hold on." Snider spoke to someone on his end. "Do we have a schematic? ... Put it on that monitor. This smacks of a single-point failure."
>
> "I'm telling you," another voice said. "All the essential systems have a backup."
>
> "Find that failure." Then Snider said to Chase, "We're losing her."
>
> "She got any thrust at all?" Chase asked.
>
> "Negative."

Now read the passage as it appears in the book. I've shown in bold text the elements that suggest differences between Chase's world and that of the reader. In some cases, these differences appear only in the language; other times they appear as descriptive details. Notice how they enhance both the dialogue and the setting.

> [Chase] activated the comm. "Morgan to tower."
>
> "Tower. Go ahead Morgan." **Director Snider's face appeared strained.** The dark rings beneath his eyes made his close-cropped, blond hair look platinum.
>
> "Tell me about the *Phoenix*."
>
> "Hold on." Snider spoke to someone Chase couldn't see. "Do we have a schematic? ... Put it on that monitor." **A man with a Stellarfare patch on the sleeve of his jumpsuit** stepped into view. Snider made room by the terminal as he spoke to the man. "This smacks of a single-point failure."
>
> "I'm telling you," the Stellarfare man said, "all the essential systems have a backup."
>
> Snider stabbed a finger at the diagram. "Find that failure." He glanced at **the holographic display that dominated the front of the small control room,** then turned to Chase. "We're losing her."
>
> "She got any thrust at all?" Chase asked.
>
> "Negative." Snider looked past the terminal. "Keep those reporters out of here." Then **the screen went dark,** disconnected at the other end.

On the second reading of each scene, find ways for your setting to affect your characters. On the third, find ways for it to affect your plot (both discussed in Chapter 4). Reread the notes you made on your setting cards. Transfer any setting-enhancement ideas to the backs of the relevant scene cards.

Rewrite Your Scenes

Before you rewrite your scenes, save your manuscript and begin working on a separate draft. If you decide later that you need something you've altered or deleted, you'll be able to retrieve the original.

During this rewrite, you'll throw away whole scenes, write new scenes, and revise some scenes so extensively you'll have to start them over from scratch. Every scene will need some form of revision. Don't let this discourage you. You must trim the fat from your first draft and bolster the weak or missing elements.

You already know what changes you need to make — you've noted them on the backs of your scene cards. Now rewrite each scene, using these notes as your guide. When you're done, review your notes to make sure you didn't skip any of the problems.

Renumber your scene cards in their new order. Add the scene length and page number to each card. You'll need it for the next step of the revision process.

Exercises

1 Select a dialogue scene you've written that contains little or no activity, like a meeting, a phone call, or a conversation inside someone's house. Think of three settings to which you might move this scene that will allow more tension or activity. Move the scene to one of these settings and rewrite it. Have someone read both versions. Ask the reader which she liked better and why.

2 Select a scene you've written. Think of five objects or actions that, if added, would illustrate the difference between your character's circumstances (the setting, the time period, the character's occupation, etc.) and your own. Rewrite the scene to incorporate at least three of these objects or actions. Have someone read both versions. Ask the reader which she liked better and why.

3 Select a scene you've written. Think of three ways in which the setting might meaningfully affect the plot or the characters. Rewrite the scene to incorporate one of these ideas. Have someone read both versions. Ask the reader which she liked better and why.

4 Do all of the above exercises using the same scene. Have someone read the original and final versions. Ask the reader which she liked better and why. You'll begin to see the difference setting can make.

7

Info

Chapters

Prologues

If you have a prologue, it should be no longer than a few manuscript pages. If it is, shorten it. Look for information you can cut or relocate within your manuscript.

In addition, your prologue should meet one or both of the following guidelines:

1   A significant span of time separates the prologue from the rest of the story. Usually the prologue is something that happened before the events in the book.

2   The viewpoint character in the prologue never appears as a viewpoint character in the rest of the book (until perhaps the epilogue).

If your prologue doesn't meet at least one of these conditions, it's not a prologue. It's either unnecessary or it's part of the story. Eliminate it or insert it as a scene elsewhere in the manuscript.

Early drafts of *Worlds Asunder* and the original plot outline for *Venus Rain* both contained prologues that failed to meet the guidelines above. I didn't want to make either scene the opening of Chapter 1 because neither was written from the hero's viewpoint. Instead, I inappropriately labeled each as a prologue.

In *Worlds Asunder*, the prologue took place in the Lunar Alpha Base traffic control room, from Director Snider's point of view. It introduced Snider, the *Phoenix* crisis, and significant elements of the setting and culture. Because it didn't meet the prologue guidelines, I cut it and moved the necessary information to other scenes.

In *Venus Rain*, the prologue took place on the surface of Venus, from the viewpoint of the hero's mother. The scene didn't have to appear first in order to work within the story, so I moved the scene to Chapter 2.

Evaluate your prologue. If it's not really a prologue, or if it's too long, correct it.

Chapter Breaks

Now decide where to put your chapter breaks. In order of increasing importance, consider these three things:

1 Make your chapters short.

I can offer no guiding principle to dictate chapter length, although you don't want your chapters to be shorter than three manuscript pages. If they are, the reader won't have time to become immersed in the story before the chapter ends. On the other hand, don't write chapters that drone on for fifty or more pages. Long chapters make the pace of your story seem slow.

The average chapter length in *Worlds Asunder* is ten manuscript pages, with a minimum of six and a maximum of eighteen. I'm not suggesting your chapters should adhere to the same average or run within the same range. This is merely an example.

However long your chapters are, shorten them near the end of the book to provide the illusion of a quickening pace. If your story naturally has a faster pace near the end, as it should, this will enhance it further.

The first twenty chapters of *Worlds Asunder* have an

average length of eleven manuscript pages. The last ten average eight pages.

Length, however, should be the least of your considerations when you define your chapter breaks.

2 Segment chapters by content.

Segmenting your chapters by content is more important than segmenting them by page count. Chapter breaks don't just divide the story; they break it down into logical pieces. Each chapter must serve a purpose within the novel.

In *Worlds Asunder*, Chapter 1 sets up Chase's external goal: finding the cause of the *Phoenix* crash. The chapter puts the case into a personal context for Chase and sets up the stakes, both personal and professional, should he fail to solve it quickly. It ends with Chase en route to the impact site.

Chapter 2 shows the recovery of the wreckage and Chase's return to the base. The chapter ends when he learns his first bit of bad news, the first complication of the case.

Chapter 3 covers a press conference in which Chase's boss pressures him to report more progress than he's actually made. The reader learns of the past failures that haunt Chase.

Summarize the purpose of each of your chapters in a similarly concise manner. You need not base them on plot events, however. They may be based on characters, locations, times, dates, etc. It all depends upon the purpose each chapter serves. Once a chapter has served its purpose, end it.

3 End with a hook.

When a reader puts your book down, he'll most likely do so at a chapter break. As such, each chapter must end with a hook strong enough to drive him onward to the next chapter.

My favorite scene ending in *Worlds Asunder* occurs when our heroes are descending a long, straight stairway toward a bunker buried deep beneath the Moon's surface. In the following passage, I've replaced the villain's name with "the villain" to preserve the mystery element for anyone who may later read the book.

> With only a few steps remaining between Chase and the room, [the villain's] familiar voice came over the speaker in Chase's helmet. "Don't be shy, Colonel. Go on in."
>
> The traitor stood at the top of the stairs with an Asian man, each wearing a pressure suit and pointing an automatic rifle. There was nowhere to run and nothing to use for cover.

Cliffhangers, like the one above, make excellent chapter endings, especially if the next chapter builds suspense by shifting to a different scene before returning to resolve the cliffhanger.

Be aware, however, that each cliffhanger must be a natural development in the story line. Otherwise your reader will recognize that you've manipulated your characters and events solely for dramatic effect.

As a counterexample, consider the following phrases, taken from the chapter endings of a critique submission:

> The last thought as I dozed off was …
>
> Just before falling asleep …
>
> I murmured my thanks for the dinner and went inside and up to my room …
>
> I gave in and took a sedative, which helped me to fall asleep.

I've received a number of critique submissions in which chapters ended with some version of, "The hero went to sleep." From the standpoint of breaking chapters logically by content, this mistake is understandable; one chapter is one day, the next chapter is the next. That's not enough, however. If your hero is in danger and passes out because somebody drugged her drink, "the hero went to sleep" might make a good cliffhanger. Otherwise, there's no hook, nothing to make the reader turn the page and begin the next chapter.

So how do you turn "the hero went to sleep" into a cliffhanger? Sometimes you've just droned on too long. Look at your last few paragraphs. Can you do without them? Would your ending the scene earlier provide a better hook? If so, delete the unnecessary paragraphs.

Alternatively, look for a point of tension in the middle of your scene (or in the middle of the scene that follows) that you can use as a cliffhanger. It's okay, sometimes preferable, to end a chapter in the middle of a scene.

In an early draft of *Worlds Asunder,* I found a chapter that ended with a form of "the hero went to sleep." To produce a cliffhanger, I moved the chapter break to appear after the opening hook of the next scene. At this point in the story, all of the physical evidence resides in an area called Hangar Three. Here's the new chapter ending:

Chase woke to a muffled boom that shook the whole of Alpha Base. He squinted at the clock, then grunted at the complaint of his joints as he rolled to his feet. 3:09 A.M. Only half-conscious, he keyed the terminal and checked the newsblips. They were reporting the latest numbers in the presidential campaign polls. Whatever had caused the disturbance, the local press hadn't responded yet. Then he tuned to the ERT alert channel. The screen flashed white letters over a red background.

ALERT: FIRE IN HANGAR BAY #3
Evacuate Delta Wing west of Corridor J

Hangar Three. The *Phoenix*!

From your scene cards, make a list of scenes. Read the last paragraph of each scene to determine how strong the hook is. You may find that some scenes don't yet have a hook. That's okay. Leave them for now. You'll fix them when we discuss scene endings in Chapter 9. On the other hand, if you find a scene that ends in a particularly strong hook, note it on your list. It's a candidate for a chapter ending.

If you find a place that needs a chapter break based on content but lacks a hook, develop one using the techniques for scene endings discussed in Chapter 9.

On your list, mark a tentative chapter break every few scenes, creating groups that seem natural based on content. Calculate how long each chapter will be. Are any significantly shorter, or longer, than the range represented by the other chapters? If so, consider shifting one or more chapter breaks by a scene or two if content considerations allow. Are chapters near the end of the book shorter, on average, than the earlier chapters? If not, re-evaluate your chapter breaks with this in mind.

When you're comfortable with the chapters you've defined, mark them on your manuscript.

Exercises

1   Choose a work of book-length fiction you're working on. Select your chapter breaks by listing your scenes and grouping them by content. Then look for a chapter that lacks an ending hook. Eliminate the final paragraph of the chapter and re-read the ending. Would this improve the hook without sacrificing the purpose of the scene? Eliminate the last two paragraphs, then the last three, and so on. Would truncating the scene improve the ending? Often it will.

2   Consider the original chapter ending from Exercise 1. Look through the scene on each side of the chapter break. Is there a moment of high tension somewhere in the middle of either scene? If you end your chapter there, would it create a cliffhanger? Without deleting any part of either scene, move the chapter break to take advantage of the moment of tension. What does this do for the effectiveness of the hook?

Exposition

At this point you have a complete, well-organized novel with believable, multi-dimensional characters, vivid settings, and a compelling plot. But the writing is essentially first draft, which means, if you're like most writers, it's crap.

Now the true revision begins. As you work through the rest of *Revising Fiction*, you'll start by looking at the bigger problems, those that encompass the entire manuscript. You'll work your way down, looking at scene structure and then at the minutiae of the text, in a paragraph-by-paragraph, word-by-word examination to seek and destroy weaknesses.

Then you'll work your way back out, reviewing each scene as a whole to make sure you haven't damaged the forest by trimming the trees. Finally, you'll look at the remaining global issues, like consistency, pacing, and format.

In this chapter, I'll discuss information-management issues, making sure you've included the right information, in the best place, in an effective manner.

Information Dumps

The three kinds of information dumps I contend with most often are technical explanations, setting descriptions, and character backstory. As a rule, include only facts being observed, heard, or considered by your viewpoint character. Doing so makes the information immediate and important. If you provide information your viewpoint character is not experiencing, it creates either a viewpoint violation or a digression. Your reader will recognize both.

So how can you manage these types of information in your manuscript?

▌   Technical explanations

Technical information (real or fictitious) can be tricky because it often comes from beyond the realm of your reader's experience. One elegant way to provide it is to have an expert character explain it to a novice.

Consider the following information dump:

> It's costly and time consuming to develop a new metal technology for use in nanochips. Manufacturing issues alone include developing processes to apply and remove the new alloy, and integrating both operations into existing manufacturing procedures, not to mention fabrication of the alloy itself, which requires the purification of all of the constituent metals and combining them into a uniform-composition material.
>
> In addition, the new metal must surpass existing technologies for at least one characteristic that's important to the manufacturer or customer, such as manufacturing cost, electrical performance, thermal response, material hardness, reliability, corrosion resistance, radiation hardness, etc...

This is a concise way to address these technical issues, and the character might even be considering these facts, which would make the information relevant. Nevertheless, you've got to make the reader care. Here's how I handled this technical download in *Worlds Asunder*.

> When Michelle arrived, she was unsure of what she was going to say. The conclusion she'd drawn was

far-fetched, to say the least, almost to the point of absurdity. She'd present her opinions, of course, but the data she'd use to support them was fairly technical and she wasn't sure how much Chase would really understand. There was also no way to know if she'd missed anything in her analysis. So she'd tell the story, just as clearly as she could, and let him decide if she was out of her mind.

This paragraph makes the reader curious about Michelle's discovery. Next, I build suspense by delaying the discussion of her findings:

She entered, carrying a thinpad full of data, and was greeted by the scent of fresh pancakes. She smiled in spite of herself and her stomach growled. Lunar pancakes were her favorite. They rose light and airy in the low gravity. There was nothing like them on Earth or even Mars.

Chase served the cakes with juice before sitting down to join her. Suddenly, she was in no hurry to broach the topic she'd come here to discuss. She knew her findings were important, through she wasn't sure how. But they could wait until after breakfast.

Throughout the meal, they discussed the investigation and the relative lack of recent progress. They'd held meetings daily since Chase rejoined the team, but the last few had been sparse in the new-information department. Then she asked Chase about his plans for retirement. They talked about his daughters until they finished breakfast and he'd cleared the dishes.

He returned to the table with two cups of coffee. "What have you got?"

Notice that I've taken this opportunity to show the comfortable relationship between these two characters and to remind the reader that their world is different from the reader's own.

I proceed with the scene's technical content only after I've piqued the reader's interest:

> She didn't know where to begin. "Well, you know we've been doing some additional tests on the chip."
>
> He nodded.
>
> "We've been trying to determine the purpose of the alloy. And the bottom line is, there isn't one."
>
> "What do you mean?" he said after a moment's pause.
>
> "I mean that someone went through the trouble and expense of developing a new metal composition for nanochip manufacturing, an alloy that nobody's ever used or experimented with before — for this purpose or any other that I can find in the literature." Her hands gestured her exasperation as she spoke. "Then they supposedly classified the process, kept it top-secret, and made sure that nobody else in the worlds has it. Am I right so far?"
>
> "Yes. Go on."
>
> "Well, they must've had a reason. **Nobody would design a technology, develop it to the point of manufacturability — which generally takes years to do** — and then classify it, **unless it was better for some application than anything already available.**"
>
> "Makes sense."
>
> She found his quiet attention encouraging. "So the guys in the lab and I have been asking ourselves the questions, 'In what way is this alloy better than

those used in the commercial sector?' and, 'To what application would that improvement best be employed?'"

"And what did you find?" He took a sip from his mug.

"I'll show you." She turned her thinpad so Chase could see the display right-side up. "We started with the obvious, **electrical characterization.** The resistivity of the alloy is slightly higher than that of the standard. For reasons of internal heating and power consumption, low resistively is categorically better than high. Then, because the chip was used for a space application, where temperatures can vary by several hundred degrees from sunlight to shade, we did a **temperature response** analysis. The response is virtually the same as that of the standard, though the melting point of the new alloy is two degrees lower."

Michelle displayed a variety of results for a wide range of physical tests, including **material hardness, reliability, corrosion resistance, and others.** She stopped to explain the significance of the various aspects of the graphical data and answered any questions that Chase asked.

It takes longer to convey the information this way, but if you get the reader caught up in the story, he won't recognize you're feeding him a large technical download. I slip from *show* to *tell* in the last paragraph to avoid getting so deep into the technical details that I lose the reader. I'll discuss the difference between showing and telling in Chapter 9.

2 Setting description

When a character first walks into a setting, don't stop the action to describe every nuance of the place. Better yet, don't stop the action at all. The original prologue of *Worlds Asunder* could have begun:

> The traffic control room was small. It had two rows of computer terminals. Behind them sat the traffic controllers, facing a central holographic display that showed the current traffic patterns. Two federal agents stood behind Director Snider. The smell of sweat hung in the air.
>
> Suddenly, an alarm sounded.

It's not a bad description. It includes three of the five senses: sight, smell, and sound. Nevertheless, it's static. Work these details into the action of the scene:

> Director Jack Snider pulled at the collar of his jumpsuit in the **sweat-fouled air of the traffic control room.** He would have paced the **aisle behind the second tier of computer terminals** if it wouldn't have betrayed his nervousness. As it was, he felt trapped. **The federal agents who stood behind him,** looking past his shoulders, made him uneasy, claustrophobic.
>
> "Something's wrong," Chavez, the controller, said. Her voice, edged with tension, carried in the **small room.**
>
> Snider's heart surged. **Trajectory traces crisscrossed the holographic display that dominated the front of the room.** The muted voices of the controllers speaking into their comm links died into silence as the trajectory displayed for the *Phoenix* turned red and separated from the green line of the ship's assigned flight path. **An alarm sounded,** reverberating off the walls and ringing in Snider's brain.

This passage isn't perfect, and it was ultimately cut from the book. It contains some *tell*:

> As it was, he felt trapped. The federal agents who stood behind him, looking past his shoulders, made him uneasy, claustrophobic.

Nevertheless, it's much better than the first example. In addition to maintaining the momentum of the story, it includes a forth sense: Snider *feels* the constriction of the confined space and his own increased heart rate.

I'll discuss setting in more detail in Chapter 9.

3   Character backstory

As you did with setting, find ways to include character backstory without stopping the action or digressing.

For example, during Chase's first case as an accident investigator, he said something to the press that he shouldn't have said. The mistake damaged a pilot's career. It's the past failure I haunt Chase with.

It just so happens that the wronged pilot from his previous case is the same pilot involved in the *Phoenix* case, the case Chase must solve in the book. This circumstance gives Chase a personal stake in the outcome, a chance for redemption. As the author, I must communicate the details of the past failure in a way that makes the information immediate, important, and engaging.

As soon as Snider assigns Chase to the case, Chase looks up the ship's records and discovers the name of the pilot:

> He read the last line again. His investigations career had come full circle, it seemed. It would end where it had begun. With Randy Lauback.

Chase knew then that he had to take the case, however long it might last, and follow it through to completion. He owed Randy that much.

This passage makes the case personal and shows the reader that Chase and Randy have a history, though it doesn't specify what that history is. It's enough for now, but at some point the reader must know the details.

The backstory seems as though it would fit into the narrative here. Unfortunately, including the information dump would slow the pace of the story — something I want to avoid, especially in the first chapter. As an author, how do I convey the details without the reader recognizing them as an information dump?

I decided to put Chase into the same situation he was in when he made the original mistake, holding a press conference with very few answers to give. Chase relives the event in his mind as he tries to do better this time. The following passage occurs just after he delivers his statement. Notice that I include the backstory as part of Chase's thoughts.

Chase went silent. He knew more, of course, but he didn't want to expose any avenues for questioning that he didn't have to. The reporters would find plenty to explore on their own. Finally he said, "I'll take your questions."

Every hand in the room went up. Chase selected a young reporter in the back, hoping that youth implied inexperience and would lead to an easy question.

"What can you say of the cause of the accident?"

The heat of the lights and the electronic eyes of the vid-scanners made Chase's body warm and his skin itchy with perspiration. On the surface, the question was easy. In fact, he'd already answered it. But it marked the beginning of a process. It was hard to stand on a pedestal, in a spotlight, in front of the nation and the worlds; hard to stand before millions of Americans who were angry at the needless deaths of four of their countrymen; hard to stand up and say, I don't know. The reporters knew that. They would ask the question again.

"It's too early in the investigation to answer that." He said the words quickly and selected another reporter.

"Can you tell us the cause of the victims' deaths?" the second reporter asked.

"Yes," Chase assured with some measure of relief. He held up the thinpad. "I was handed the preliminary coroner's report just a few minutes ago. Lauback, Conway, and Herrera died from asphyxiation. Their O_2 tanks were empty when we found them. They ran out of air."

"And Agent Lederman?" the reporter asked.

The report on Lederman also said asphyxiation, but listed the determination as speculative. According to an appended comment, the condition of the body made the evaluation "problematic."

But to Chase, it didn't make sense. Lederman's air tank was full when they found him. Could he have been a victim of his own gun? Chase made a mental note to discuss it with the coroner. "The cause of Lederman's death is still undetermined. His body was exposed to space. That complicates the autopsy."

Chase selected a reporter in the front row.

"Is it true that the data core was damaged?"

"Yes, but it still contains valuable information." He acknowledged another reporter.

"Obviously the investigation's just getting started, and you've yet to draw your conclusions, but can you name any possible contributors to the incident, based on the evidence you've seen?"

There it was again. They'd push a little further each time they asked until they forced him into a corner that he couldn't talk himself out of. *I don't know. I don't know. I don't know.* The mantra wailed like a siren in his mind. He searched for the courage to say it out loud.

His thoughts went back to his first case. **He'd been unable to say it then, so he'd speculated. The North Star fire had started somewhere in the cockpit before liftoff, during preflight.**

"Could the pilot have performed the preflight checks incorrectly?" a reporter had asked.

"Yes," Chase had answered. He didn't know whether he had or not, but he could have.

The reporter mistook the response as a finding of blame against the pilot.

That pilot was Randy Lauback.

Chase had realized his blunder only after the newsblips filled with accusations of guilt against Randy, whose flight license was immediately revoked. Chase hadn't wanted to correct the statement until he was sure it was wrong. It shouldn't have taken more than a few days to prove one way or the other. But it was weeks later when he discovered the faulty wiring that had sparked the flames, which had spread rapidly in the oxygen-rich cockpit. Randy was innocent.

In the meantime, the press had repeated the original accusation with damning regularity. And although Randy regained his license, his reputation never recovered.

Chase still hadn't forgiven himself for that

mistake, but he had no way to make it right. He'd even tried to persuade the networks to run a retraction and apology. But the public didn't care, so neither did the press. Now, with the *Phoenix* case, he might make some small form of recompense.

In the room before him, the reporters became restless as they waited for Chase to respond.

"It would be inappropriate for me to speculate at this time." He'd learned much about the media in the last four years.

This passage shows the pressure Chase feels whenever he's in the public spotlight and how that pressure caused him to mishandle his first press conference. It shows that he learned from his mistake and has grown as a character, that he's striving to do better, and why it's important to him that he do so. Furthermore, it shows all this at a time when Chase is thinking about it. It's still an information dump, but even if the reader recognizes it as such, the importance of the information will be obvious.

Read through your manuscript for information dumps. Find creative ways to include the information without stopping the story. Deliver it in character.

Misplaced Information

Introduce information when its importance is obvious to the reader; otherwise he'll skip or skim the passage. If you've introduced something in scene two, for example, that's not important until scene eight, move it to scene eight. If it's never important, cut it.

The following passage is from the beginning of a critique submission:

The small transport hopper fired its retro engines in preparation for landing. Tridia Odana, strapped securely into a passenger seat, tried to anticipate the craft's landing, but was nevertheless jolted as it settled onto the landing pad. Just another sign of exhaustion, she thought to herself. She remained seated for some time after the engines had stilled, preparing her mind for the onrush of activity awaiting her inside the check-in station.

The station was always bustling, and a crowd of people meant a bombardment of thoughts to block from her consciousness. Tridia was seventeen, extremely intelligent, and telepathic. A soldier in a mercenary army — one of its elite — and she was returning from a Challenge mission that had earned her a promotion in the Hierarchy's Challenge Grid. It had been a difficult mission that she deliberately took to the limit of her time and endurance. She challenged three men to capture her in the desert-environment training grounds, dangling before them the chance to best the only unbeaten lieutenant in the Challenge Grid, as well as retrieve damaging evidence they could not afford to have fall into the hands of the Hierarchy's Tribunal. The men were vicious and tenacious, but she had turned the tables on them easily enough. The hunters became the prey under the watchful eyes of the desert moons and more than a dozen strategically placed satellites. She led them over dunes, up rock climbs and through gullies, taunting them along while staying just out of reach. In the end, when her water ran out and the scorching sun threatened to drain the last of her strength, she doubled back, herded them into a blind arroyo and picked them off with her stun weapon. They were bound and loaded into the prisoner's locker of the transport hopper long before the effects of the stun wore off. Unfortunately, the trip back to the Rodan Base check-in station took several hours and the men, upon awakening, ranted and raved, thinking thoughts that caused Tridia physical pain to control.

With her mind fully occupied blocking out the anger and rage she sensed coming from the prisoner locker, she miscalculated the landing and was jolted. A small thing in itself, but an indication of her deteriorating faculties. With her eyes closed, she braced her mind for what lay ahead.

You didn't read the whole second paragraph, did you? That's okay. This entire paragraph is misplaced information. It stops the action. It's *tell*. And although Tridia's backstory may be important, she has no reason to ponder it at this particular moment. The author should cut the paragraph and include any necessary information in a later scene.

Look for misplaced information in your manuscript. Move it to where it belongs, even if that's a separate document titled "Deleted Passages."

Repeated Information

Your reader needs to be told things only once, or better yet, never *told* and *shown* only once. As writers, we tend to repeat ourselves, either because we've forgotten what we've already said or to remind the reader of an earlier point.

In either case, purge the repeats. Read your manuscript, beginning to end, with this in mind. When you find information you think you may repeat later, or see something you know you've said before, highlight it. Then go back and read the highlighted sections. If you've repeated yourself by mistake, choose the best place to include the information and delete it everywhere else.

If you repeated yourself for the sake of emphasis or because you fear the reader may have forgotten something, don't. Give the reader some credit. If the importance of the information was obvious the first time, he'll remember it. If it wasn't, delete the passage and go with the second, or the third, etc.

In the example above, the third paragraph contains a lot of information repeated from the first. I suggested the author rewrite these paragraphs to preserve the best parts of both:

Tridia Odana endured the confinement of a passenger seat on the small transport hopper until it finally fired its retro engines and slowed for landing. Her mind was so occupied blocking the rage emanating from the prisoners' locker that she was jolted by the bump of the ship's settling onto the landing pad. Just another sign of exhaustion. She closed her eyes as the engines stilled and braced her mind for the onrush of activity waiting inside the station.

This passage gives the reader a hint about the special nature of Tridia's mind without saying she's telepathic, a fact that will become clear soon enough. It reveals the genre of the story (science fiction) and makes the reader curious about Tridia. (Who is she? Why is she exhausted? Who are the prisoners?) Furthermore, the passage contains little or no repeated information.

Revealing Character

This section takes a closer look at character information. Because your characters are the heart of your story, the way you present them deserves a second, more critical, look. Read your manuscript and make sure the reader learns about your characters little by little through their thoughts, actions, dialogue, and emotions, rather than all at once through narration.

Consider the following excerpt from an early draft of *Worlds Asunder*:

Edward "Chase" Morgan was an accident investigator for NASA. He'd retired from the air force as a colonel nearly twenty years before. Having gone into the military straight out of high school, he retired young and later enjoyed an exciting career as an astronaut. He trained hard and earned a position on several deep-space missions. He had seen most of the solar system, including Mars, Jupiter, and even an exploratory mission all the way out to Pluto and Charon. Four years ago, he gave up the stick for a job in the Office of Accident Investigation and had been assigned to Lunar Alpha base. His career was winding down and he was simply getting too old to be gallivanting among the worlds.

He was a black man of average height and trim build, with curly gray hair and beard. Most would simply describe him as old and skinny. His manner was calm and imperturbable.

This passage certainly tells the reader who he is and what he looks like. The problem is, it stops the action and *tells* the reader who he is and what he looks like. The goal is to *show* the reader who he is and who he perceives himself to be (which might be two different things) without stopping the action. During the revisions, I strove to achieve this goal.

In the opening scene, Chase tells Michelle Fairchild a story about a night he spent partying with his air force buddies. After the story, Michelle says:

"I can't picture you drunk."

To this Chase replies:

"I haven't been drunk since **I retired from the air force twenty years ago.**"

This reveals what the reader needs to know about Chase's time in the air force and suggests his approximate age. More important, however, is Chase's NASA history:

Chase cleared the remnants of dinner and poured himself another cup of coffee. The gold watch that Director Jack Snider had given him at his **twentieth employment-anniversary ceremony the previous night** was still sitting on the counter. Chase took out the watch and returned to the table.

The **NASA** inscription across the top offset the **Lunar Alpha Base** logo beneath the display. Nowhere did it say, **"Office of Accident Investigations."** Maybe Snider recognized that Chase didn't belong in Investigations. **He'd been put there after he lost his flight status four years ago because he was too old to do anything else.**

This version contains most of the same information about Chase's NASA career yet delivers it with greater subtlety and from within Chase's thoughts.

I broke the remaining information into pieces, which I included as opportunities arose. The following passage shows his appearance and reveals, however briefly, the calm demeanor he demonstrates throughout the novel:

The comm panel buzzed. Chase stretched his **lanky frame** and got to his feet, then leapt to the terminal against the slight lunar g.

He keyed the link. On the screen, a frown elongated the narrow face of Security Chief Stan Brower, whose sharp eyes were nearly as pale as his graying hair. This wouldn't be good news.

"We've got a ship in trouble," Brower said. "The *Phoenix*. Snider needs you to assemble a team."

"The *Phoenix*?"

"A freighter. Belongs to Stellarfare. She was on her way from here to Montanari when she lost thrust, but it looks like she might come back around toward Alpha … if they don't regain control."

"You don't sound like you think they will."

"No reason to."

Chase ran an **ebony hand** through **his hair**, which had **turned gray, along with his mustache and beard,** years ago. "Any reason to think they won't?"

The remark about Chase's deep-space missions appears in a couple of ways:

As he killed the link, Chase tried to imagine what the crew must be going through. **During his own deep-space missions,** he'd experienced a number of technical glitches. They were nothing short of terrifying, but he had never had a loss of thrust. Usually you had options, but not without thrust. Nothing could make a pilot feel so powerless.

And later, as Chase ponders the effect his time away has had on his family:

By that time, Erin had been away at college. She'd been more mature and independent than Sarah; she hadn't been around to watch her mother fall apart, and she'd understood better her father's compulsion to push the envelope, to be **the first black man to venture past Saturn, and the first human to orbit Pluto and Charon.** Erin hadn't forsaken him.

Now, instead of being told everything about Chase in the first two paragraphs of his introduction, the reader gets to know him over time. They're still learning about him, and he about himself, right up to the end of the book.

Strive to achieve this in your manuscript.

Exercises

1   Find a scene in which you've introduced technical information or cultural background. Consider how you've presented the information. Is it immediately important to the characters and relevant to the events in the scene? Is it there because the viewpoint character is thinking about it, seeing it, hearing it, or otherwise experiencing it? Or have you stopped the action to explain it? Delete any information that's not immediately important or that the viewpoint character isn't experiencing. If it's important, find a way to bring it to the mind of your viewpoint character. Find ways to work in the information without stopping the action of the scene. Rewrite the scene, and then have someone read both versions. Ask the reader which she liked better and why.

2   Find a scene in which you've introduced a setting for the first time. Did you stop the action to describe it? If so, find ways to include the important details without stopping the action. Rewrite the scene, and then have someone read both versions. Ask the reader which she liked better and why.

3   Find a scene in which you've provided character backstory. Is the information immediately important to the characters and relevant to the events in the scene? Is the information there because the viewpoint character is thinking about it? Or have you stopped the action to provide the backstory? Look for ways to bring the backstory to your character's mind in a way that makes its importance obvious to the reader. Rewrite the scene, and then have someone read both versions. Ask the reader which she liked better and why.

9

Scenes

It's time to narrow your focus. In this chapter, you'll look at the most important building blocks of your novel: your scenes. As you examine each, edit for only one thing at a time, but don't go on to the next scene until you've edited the current scene for each potential problem discussed in this chapter.

Scene Structure

Each scene must be a story in its own right. Read each scene and make sure it contains all of the following elements:

1. A hook that draws the reader into the scene
2. A goal for the characters to accomplish
3. An obstacle between the characters and their goal
4. Action performed by the characters to overcome the obstacle
5. Some reaction in response to the characters' action
6. A problem leading into the next scene

If your scene doesn't have all these elements, you haven't written a scene. You may have written part of a scene or you may have written a summary of events. Develop the passage or combine it with another to create a scene. Otherwise, cut it and move any important information or events to another scene.

Scene Openings

Every scene must open with a hook that will draw the reader into the scene. Consider this opening paragraph from a critique submission:

> It was a filthy little joint, hidden among the shadows on the south side of Albuquerque. Jason wasn't quite sure what the attraction was to the scores of teenagers who chose the club as their hangout, but that didn't matter. The food there was good. Not the food on the menu, oh no, that stuff was horrid. The *other* food.

The author sets the scene in this paragraph, but all we get is setting. Notice how much more effectively the opening hooks the reader if she adds just three words.

> It was a filthy little joint, hidden among the shadows on the south side of Albuquerque. Jason wasn't quite sure what the attraction was to the scores of teenagers who chose the club as their hangout, but that didn't matter. The food there was good. Not the food on the menu, oh no, that stuff was horrid. The other food. **The vampire food.**

Now she has put a vampire in a club full of teenagers. The reader will want to know what happens next.

The following examples are scene openings from *Worlds Asunder.*

> The transport came into the open and turned broadside to the geology team. Seconds later, all hell broke loose. Holes perforated the right side of the transport and a whirlwind of air rushed out. Sparks flew, equipment shattered, men screamed, and bullets ricocheted throughout the compartment.

This is the whizzing-bullet hook. Use it only if the remainder of the scene warrants the intensity you've given the hook. With it, you make a promise that the scene will be intense and edge-of-your-seat exciting. You must keep that promise. I'll come back to this scene later, when I talk about building tension.

Most of the time, your hook won't involve whizzing bullets, just something to tease the reader into having a go at the rest of the scene:

> When Chase entered the conference room the following day, he felt tension in the air. Everyone was there — Snider, Brower, Forsythe, the techs, analysts, and administrators — all silent and brooding amid the sterile décor of aluminite paneling. The excitement of the device discovery had worn off and everyone seemed to sense a change in the course of the investigation.

This hook is more subdued. No bullets, just our hero walking into a room. Notice how my description of the setting, and the people in it, foreshadows a turning point in the plot. The reader will want to know what it is.

Compelling dialogue can also make an effective hook:

> "Sabotage? Are you sure?" Snider said when Chase reported later that day.

This line hooks the reader because it invalidates the underlying assumption that the characters have been working with: that the *Phoenix* crash was an accident. The reader will want to know what they'll do about it.

Use dialogue hooks carefully. Don't backtrack later to explain the context of the spoken line. In the example above, the dialogue tag provides all the context the reader needs. If you must do more than that to set up the context, do it before the dialogue.

Here's another hook, one that introduces an interesting new character:

Major Bill Ryan tossed his duffel bag into the back seat of his cherry Calypso convertible and checked his watch. Damn. He pulled his tall, well-honed body into the driver's seat and turned the key even before he was fully settled behind the wheel. Tires chirped on the pavement as he pulled away from the curb. You'd think that sixteen years in the air force would've taught him punctuality.

There are many ways to draw your reader into a scene. Make sure every scene has some form of opening hook.

Show and Tell

Never tell something you can show. This is a difficult concept for many new writers, but it's crucial. It lurks beneath many of the problems discussed throughout this book, from information dumps (Chapter 8), to building tension (later in this chapter), to passive voice and filter words (Chapter 11). Telling the story, rather than showing it, gives it the detached feel of a news article. It prevents the reader from experiencing it as though she's the viewpoint character. It leeches the importance, the very life, out of the events.

The question is, how do you know if you're showing or telling? My rule of thumb is simple.

You may state facts:

Gerri threw the contract onto the floor, snatched up her coat and stormed from the room.

But don't draw conclusions for your reader:

Gerri was angry.

In the first sentence, you see Gerri's actions, and are allowed to draw your own conclusion that she's angry. This is *show*. In the second, I've drawn the conclusion for you. This is *tell*. Decide for yourself which is more compelling to read.

Here are some examples from a critique submission. The scene is written from the viewpoint of a teenage boy named Ian.

Tell:

> There was someone breaking into the house.

Show:

> The trapdoor burst down and Ian jumped backwards. Dust showered the cardboard boxes that cluttered the closet floor. As soon as the ladder thunked down, a black boot stepped onto the top rung, followed by another.

Here's an example from the next sentence of the same critique submission.

Tell:

> [Ian's] first thought was that he should probably get help, but he was much too distracted.

Show:

> ... before [Ian] could run for help, the shapely legs of the woman in the boots arrested him.

Ian fails to move because of the intruder's attractive legs. This shows that he's distracted without saying, "He was distracted." The phrase "before he could run for help" shows Ian's thoughts without saying, "He thought he should get help."

Here's an example in which the same author did a delightful job of showing:

> [Rhiannon] leaned forward, her eyes fixed on the artery that had begun to pulse faster as she leaned close to it ...

This is a great line. It shows the emotions of both characters. Rhiannon, whom you've already surmised is a vampire, leans forward with her eyes fixed on Ian's pulsing artery. It's absolutely clear what she wants, and the author never said, "Rhiannon was hungry for blood." Ian's artery pulsing faster shows his fear or excitement (context suggests that he's feeling more of the latter) without saying, "He was afraid," or "He was excited."

Examine your scenes for passages that tell, rather than show. Be particularly attentive to places where you do any of the following:

- Provide a lot of description, such as of a culture, situation, or technology
- Introduce a character or place
- Present a rapid string of events
- Have a jump in time
- Provide a bridge between events
- Supply character backstory[1]

Rewrite any sections in which you've told something. To find a way to show it, I ask myself this question: What can the viewpoint character see, hear, feel, smell, taste, or recall, that allows him to draw the conclusions that I've told instead of shown? In other words, how does he know this? If you've drawn a conclusion for the reader, the viewpoint character must also have drawn this conclusion. On what is his conclusion based?

If the viewpoint character has nothing upon which to base the conclusion, no way to know the thing you've told, then the section of *tell* constitutes a viewpoint violation. Delete it or find some other place in your manuscript to reveal the information. Keep in mind, though, if you move it, it's still *tell*. You must still convert it to *show*.

Having said that, there are times when *tell* will serve you well.

▌ Short, occasional bits of *tell* can help keep the story from jumping, seemingly haphazardly, from scene to scene.

In the following example from *Worlds Asunder*, the reader hasn't seen the characters for several scenes, during which two days of story time have passed. I had to account for the time without going into a long, blow-by-blow scene showing two days of unimportant happenings.

Then, two days into their stay, Bill managed to separate Dana from the guys so he could enjoy some time alone with her, which he hadn't been able to do since their first night on the base. They went to the Tranquility Restaurant, which he favored for its reasonable prices — by lunar standards — quiet atmosphere, and the subtly masculine, romantic feel of the burgundy and brass decor.

Neither had mentioned what had happened in his quarters. It was safer not to. There never seemed to be any repercussions from his advances as long as he didn't press them.

"It's nice to have a bit of a break." Dana dug into her vegetable lasagna.

"From the training schedule, or from the guys?"

This is followed by a page and a half of dialogue that constitutes about five minutes of story time. The two opening paragraphs of *tell* give the reader a context for the dialogue and enhance the continuity of the characters, a sense that Bill and Dana carry on with their lives even when they don't appear on the page.

2   Some events aren't important enough to justify a full scene.

In the following example, Chase investigates the origin of an important piece of electronic hardware:

That done, he went back to his apartment and spent the rest of the morning and most of the afternoon on the telnet with NASA's Earthbound investigations branch.

Almost immediately, they determined that the chip was Chinese, not Japanese, and that the text on the package translated into a product

**code and serial number. That was promising. If
they could determine who made the chip, they
might be able to track it to a customer, and from
there, to the person who planted it. They sifted
through the data from China's many nanoelec-
tronics manufacturers, but by mid-afternoon,
they'd gotten nowhere.** "Keep trying," Chase told
his colleagues. "Somebody made that chip."

These two paragraphs are almost entirely *tell.* One
critiquer suggested I expand them into a scene and
show the conversation that took place. I considered
doing this, but because the effort to track the com-
ponent back to a manufacturer was, for the moment,
fruitless, I didn't feel it justified a scene. Ultimately, I
left the passage as *tell.*

As a counterexample, an early draft of *Worlds Asunder*
contained the following text, right after Chase discovers
signs of sabotage:

**He went immediately to inform Director
Snider of the finding. It would change the face
of the investigation for both NASA and the
press.**

A critiquer called me on this, and rightly so. The second sentence of this passage states that this is an important development in the plot, much too important to
gloss over in just a few lines. I expanded the passage into
a scene that shows Snider's reaction and the dialogue
that ensues.

3 Use narrative summary (*tell*) to avoid repeating events
you've already shown.

Mariano motioned to one of his aides, a man of maybe twenty-five years. The aide slipped a data card into a slot in the table and keyed the first image. A hologram of Lunar Alpha Base appeared over the emitter in the center of the table. "Ladies and gentlemen." The speaker shifted his weight from one foot to the other. "The People's Republic of China has made a series of deliberate and successful attacks on several United States interests located on the Moon. First, the Stellarfare freighter *Phoenix* and the US energy secretary. Second, NASA's Lunar Alpha Base and the federal agent investigating the first attack. And yesterday, the Fusion Resource Corporation and the new helium plant at the Montanari mine."

He spent the next ten minutes cycling through a series of holograms related to each attack.

In this passage from *Worlds Asunder*, the last sentence is *tell*. Showing this would require me to include the monologue of the aide's presentation, monologue that would relate the details of three events I've already spent page after page, scene after scene, showing. Because the reader can recall those scenes, telling that the aide presented the details serves my purpose much better than showing would.

Showing Emotions

Telling emotions is such a common problem that it's worth discussing separately. In some ways, the telling of emotions is easier to identify than other forms of *tell*. Read your scenes and look for the name of any emotion:

He felt **defensive**.
Chase was **relieved**.
It **concerned** him.

Consider the following passage from an early draft of *Worlds Asunder*.

Dana spent most of the day after Bill's surgery sitting at his bedside, battling a tumult of unfamiliar emotions. Frustration at her helplessness, fear that she'd lose her best friend, anger at those who had done this to him, regret for never having expressed her feelings in any meaningful way, and sadness for the loss of her fallen companions.

This *tells* what Dana is feeling. The revised passage below *shows* the same emotions:

Dana spent most of the day after Bill's surgery sitting at his bedside. The doctors and nurses came and went, but she didn't talk to them, afraid her voice would fail her if she did. Instead, she watched their faces and tried to read Bill's progress in their expressions [fear of losing her friend].

She'd lost her friends and her innocence, taken by an enemy upon whom she'd fired the first shot [sadness and regret]. So she buried her head in her hands to block out everything from her sight but the man she was helpless to aid [helplessness].

Anger and frustration are missing from the second passage. I decided they would have faded to the background, supplanted by deeper, more profound feelings. Besides, the original passage contained too many emotions to begin with.

If you're having difficulty determining whether you've told or shown an emotion, find a way to portray it without using the name of the emotion or a synonym. You can't *tell* an emotion without using its name or a synonym.

The telling of emotions may be easy to spot, but for many writers, it's one of the most difficult to correct. The following techniques will help you effectively show your characters' emotions.

1 Use emotional honesty.

Emotions are complex, and each is part of an emotional spectrum. The passage above that shows Dana sitting at Bill's bedside is a good example of the complexity of human emotions. Don't restrict your characters to one emotion at a time or to emotional extremes.

2 Understand the source of the character's emotion and communicate it to the reader.

Consider the following passage:

> Several minutes passed. Dana's chest tightened with each passing second. It was nothing, she told herself. She should have expected it. But she was sweating in her pressure suit.

Clearly, Dana is worried about something, or something bad and unexpected has happened; the reader can't be sure which. Though I've shown Dana's physical response to her emotion, the emotion itself is lost.

Here's the revised passage:

> Several minutes passed. Still no word came. Dana's chest tightened with each passing second. It was nothing, she told herself. Bill was always late. She should have expected it. But she was sweating in her pressure suit.

More minutes passed. *Come on, Bill*. The mission was timed to bring down the first four targets in the first two minutes of the attack. Yet no report came from the *Puma*.

The reader now knows what Dana's worried about and why. Show the cause, and the emotion becomes real.

3   Avoid clichés.

Mad as hell
Green with envy
Love so much it hurts
Hate with a passion

Overused phrases like these may *tell* the reader what your character feels, but they don't allow him to experience what your character is going through. Simply put, they don't *show*. Find more original ways to express your characters' emotions.

4   Use concrete details.

Not bugs, but locusts and flies. Not flowers, but crocuses, pansies, or marigolds. If your character is drinking soda or wine, name the brand (real or fictitious). If she's reading a book or listening to a song, name it. Choose details that reflect your character's emotional state.

Consider the following passage, from an early draft of *Worlds Asunder*, in which Dana McKaughey first visits Bill Ryan in the hospital:

Tubes and wires ran everywhere, to machines and equipment whose purpose she could only guess at.

Does this passage let you feel what Dana's feeling? No. It shows her ignorance of the equipment sustaining Bill, but it doesn't convey emotion. Because she's not familiar with the machines, I can't describe them by name or function, but I can give details to the extent that she understands them:

> Tubes and wires ran everywhere, from his arm, mouth, nose, chest, and several from beneath a blanket that had been pulled down to his waist. Each connected him to equipment in his headboard.
>
> Meaningless numbers and graphics lit the display. She heard the hollow pump and hiss of a respirator and a series of beeps with the rhythm of a steady heart, but she'd cautioned herself against false hope for too many hours to draw encouragement from the disembodied sounds.

Instead of wires just running everywhere, they now run from specific parts of Bill's body to equipment in his headboard. Instead of settling for "machines and equipment," I describe what Dana sees and hears in a manner that reflects her emotions.

5 Use internal monologue.

This example is from Bill Ryan in *Worlds Asunder*:

> Why couldn't he share *that* part of her life? Whenever he tried, she was just responsive enough to make him think he had a chance. But in the end, she always kept him at arm's length.
>
> But Bill had resolved years ago not to psychoanalyze her behavior. He reminded himself of that pledge now to prevent his mind from slipping into

that self-destructive mire of a woman's emotional logic. Women's prerogative, he repeated over and over again to make himself believe it. Some days it got to him more than others.

This shows more about his emotional state, and about him as a character, than words like *frustration* or *loneliness* could possibly convey.

6   Use dialogue.

This example is from a critique submission:

> [Ian] reached the table just in time to get the last slice of mushrooms, olives, and green chili, much to the annoyance of his sister.

The author could have used dialogue to *show* the girl's annoyance:

> [Ian] reached the table just in time to get the last slice of mushrooms, olives, and green chili.
> "Mom," Kasey yelled in her most whiney voice. "Ian took the last piece of good pizza."
> "You're a kid. You're not even supposed to like these toppings." Ian made a show of stuffing half the piece into his mouth in a single bite.
> "Mom," Kasey yelled again.

The second passage reveals both characters much more clearly than the first, which simply tells the reader that Kasey is annoyed. The second passage shows, through dialogue, how both characters respond to her annoyance.

7   Have the character respond to the emotion in an unexpected way.

Snider pulled Chase aside. "That was a lovely exercise," he spat, "but you haven't answered the basic question: why?" Veins bulged in his forehead as he said the last word. His eyes, crazed as though he was on the verge of a breakdown, spoke of the unbelievable pressure that he must be under. Chase had thought he'd understood, but matters were apparently worse than he'd imagined.

"Look, Morgan." Snider dropped his voice. "You must answer that question. And soon. I'm getting to the point where I don't even care if it's the right answer." He looked Chase in the eye. "You hear what I'm saying?"

In this example, Snider responds to his stress by essentially telling Chase to lie. This is surprising, because Snider's primary concern has been his own reputation, which could be ruined by such a lie.

This technique can be tricky to employ because the emotional response must be believable, even though it's unexpected. The key is to make it specific to the character. I do this here by incorporating one of Snider's identifying lines: "You hear what I'm saying?"

8 Use one emotion to express another.

The following day they received a broken transmission from Snider, crackling through a faulty connection in the comm gear. A pair of geologists had arrived on the scene and found Herrera's bodyguard dead in the cabin. Chase swallowed hard and bowed his head for a moment ...

"Everyone else is missing," Snider finished.

The news was good and bad. It reminded Chase of the fragility of life and the cold ruthlessness of space. And he mourned the loss, even though he hadn't known the man. But according to Snider's report, the rover was still moving. Somehow the others had found the means to endure without the protection of a ship or habitat.

In this example, I talk about mourning over the man found in the wreckage, but because Chase didn't know the man, there's no basis for his grief. What he's actually feeling is hope for those who still live. The mention of mourning is a way to express Chase's hope by contrasting it with another, dissimilar, emotion.

9   Show physical response.

The bodies, when he found them, were nothing more than a partial set of scorched bones and ash, incompletely cremated, with a few melted personal effects. Bile filled Chase's throat and forced him to turn away. Damn it! Nobody was supposed to be in there. The death count was now at six, and Chase had known some of those people. He swallowed the vomit that rose in him, fortified his resolve, and looked again upon the victims. Both skulls remained intact, their bony grins mocking him from the ruins of his investigation. He imagined the perpetrator doing the same from somewhere nearby.

This passage uses the involuntary response of Chase's body to express his revulsion. Without it, the scene contains some macabre imagery, but it's emotionally lifeless.

10   Use external setting to mirror your character's emotions.
      In the following example, Bill has just awoken from a coma. Dana has stepped away from his bedside to allow

the nurse to assess his condition. Notice how I use the sunlight in the hospital room to reflect Dana's feelings:

> The sun warmed the room through the durapane window, suddenly now bright and cheerful as if it had just risen. Dana returned to Bill's side and kissed him again, this time on the mouth. "I thought I'd lost you."

11 Use character action.

> Chase stood, shoved his chair into the wall, and stormed from the room.

In this example from *Worlds Asunder*, Chase's anger is obvious from his actions.

12 Express the emotion in a way that is specific to the character.

> [President Powers] felt like she had when she was twelve, when she and her friends were playing in the surf off the South Carolina coast. She'd waded in a little too far and a particularly large wave washed over her, pulled her under.
>
> China armed in Earth orbit and the United States ignorant. She couldn't breathe. A cold pressure squeezed in around her, holding her down while she was powerless to prevent it. She heard Norton slam the table through the muffled sound that filled her ears. They were arguing, Norton and O'Leary, but only Norton's voice penetrated the president's consciousness with the words *incompetent* and *consequences*.
>
> Finally, like it had when she was twelve, the wave receded and she came up for air. She banged her

cane on the hardwood floor to bring civility back to the meeting.

In this example, I use a specific event from President Powers' childhood to express her sense of being overwhelmed in a way that is specific to her.

13   Use comparisons.

In the following passage, Dana has spent the past several hours in the trauma center waiting for news on Bill's condition:

> Finally, Bill's doctor emerged from the surgical wing wearing a white smock that looked like it had never been worn before. He was an angel or an apparition, his face devoid of any emotion that might reveal the state of his patient. Dana might have imagined him. Nonetheless, she rushed forward.

The comparison of the doctor to an angel or an apparition, two disparate beings, shows the complexity of Dana's emotions. Her action in the final sentence shows that her hope is stronger than her fear.

For a more in-depth treatment of this topic, I refer you to *Creating Character Emotions*, by Ann Hood.

Anachronism

Anachronism (the presence of persons, objects, events, or even words that are chronologically out of place) can manifest itself in many ways in your manuscript. The most obvious is a technology that's inappropriate to your time period. You may have included some gadget before its time, like a cellular phone in a story that takes place in the 1970's. In this example, the technology's not far from its time, but the astute reader will catch it. It will detract from the realism of the story and damage your credibility as a writer. Research your time period. Know the technology of the era.

This works in reverse for science fiction. If your story takes place in the future. Don't include a technology from the past, especially if it's outdated today. If you include a technology from the present, ask yourself if it's likely to evolve between now and the time in which your story takes place. If so, how?

Scene Endings

Your scene ending is the reader's reward for having read the scene. It should do two things: wrap up the scene in a way that satisfies the reader, and compel him to begin the next scene.

To do this, your scene should end in one of the following ways:

1   Cliffhanger (preferably followed by a jump cut)

During the "Organization" section of Chapter 6, I mentioned adding one line to the middle of an action scene in *Worlds Asunder* to create a cliffhanger. In that scene, the heroes are fighting their way through the enemy stronghold. Hostile gunmen cover the corridor before them when their way back is suddenly cut off. I added the following line:

> They no longer had a choice. They had to run the gauntlet. [End of scene and chapter]

Get your hero into trouble, then leave your reader hanging.

2   Revealing internal monologue

In one *Worlds Asunder* scene, Chase loses the *Phoenix* case to a federal agent named Forsythe. I might have ended this scene with:

> Chase left the meeting and went home.

How does Chase feel about losing control of the case? You'd never know from the passage above, which provides no incentive for the reader to turn the page. Watch what happens when I use revealing internal monologue to let the reader into Chase's mind:

> When Chase left the meeting an hour later, he felt a hollow ache inside. He wandered the tall corridors of the base, sifting through his feelings. **He'd been in charge of his own activities for decades. The autonomy of the Office of Accident Investigations, like that of deep-space flight, had allowed him a freedom of action that he'd miss under Forsythe's direction. As his loss of flight status had been four years before, this was one more step toward the inadequacy and dependence that defined old age.**

This passage occurs early in the book and reveals the starting point of Chase's character arc, that old age has made him feel inadequate and dependent. In addition, Chase has a personal need to solve the case himself. This paragraph shows what losing control of it does to him emotionally. The reader will want to know what he's going to do about it.

3   Emotional dialogue

In this example, Bill Ryan, the commander of the *Puma*, has failed to return from a combat mission. The scene, written from Dana's viewpoint, could have ended like this:

> "If there's a chance they're still alive," Snider said, "then they deserve every effort we can make to help them. In the meantime, Robinson, try to raise the *Puma* on the comm."

This passage tries to be a hook because Bill remains unaccounted for at the end of the scene. This ending offers the reader too much hope, however, so I added the following paragraphs:

> Dana moved to the window and looked down at the bustle of activity on the launch pad. The *Snow Leopard* looked small and fragile from up here as it disappeared into the hangar. Her gaze drifted out over the horizon to the stars and she started to cry.
>
> Johnny Miller put a reassuring hand on her shoulder, gave her a cup of coffee, and said nothing. He didn't tell her that they could be wrong. He didn't promise that Bill was all right.
>
> Dana held the cup dumbly before her. "I never told him that I loved him."

Here the reader discovers Dana's feelings for Bill. The passage raises the stakes and dampens the hope. It creates the suspense necessary for an effective hook.

Digressions

In Chapter 6, you examined your manuscript for entire scenes that failed to move the plot forward or reveal character. Look for the same problem in the passages within each scene. Cut any paragraph, or even sentence, that doesn't advance the plot or reveal some aspect of character.

Scene Length

Read your scene for length. As with chapters, there are no hard and fast rules for the lengths of scenes, provided that they contain all of the elements a scene should have (discussed earlier in this chapter). *Worlds Asunder* contains scenes as short as one manuscript page and as long as fifteen.

Having said that, a scene should be short if it relies primarily on exposition — an information dump of background or plot information — if it contains a lot of scenic description, or if it's an erotic scene. It should be longer if it's a conversation, an emotional scene, or a suspenseful scene.[2]

Building Tension

The difference between suspense and tension is duration. Suspense should be maintained throughout the story. Tension is momentary, lasting for seconds or minutes. Suspense makes the reader want to know what will happen next. Tension makes her heart race.[3]

Take every opportunity to increase the tension in your scenes. In an early draft of *Worlds Asunder*, I came across the following passage, in which Chase tumbles from the back of a flatbed cargo truck driven by the villain:

Action

Tells what's happening in the story

> The truck sped forward. This time he rolled off the back into the dirt, and the truck raced ahead without him. The crack in his visor was now a hand's width long. He checked his suit's pressure gauge. It was holding, but not for long, and his air was almost gone.
>
> He pulled the rifle to his shoulder and took aim at the departing truck. It was several hundred meters away, but that wasn't far. With two shots, he took out the left rear tire. The right rear went three shots later. The drive wheels sank into the fine sand and the truck ground to a halt.

What's wrong with this passage? Quite simply, it lacks tension. The content should be exciting. It's the climactic scene of the story: The hero is on the Moon, he's been thrown from the back of a truck, his air is almost gone, his oxygen tank is leaking, his faceplate is cracked, he's in the middle of nowhere, he has no transportation, and the bad guy is getting away. Yet all I had to say was, "He pulled the rifle to his shoulder and took aim at the departing truck."

Worse, when I said the truck was several hundred meters away, I downplayed the problem by adding, "but that wasn't far." Never downplay the problem. Build it up. Make everything a big deal.

I'm writing from Chase's point of view. The reader must feel his desperation. She must feel the tension:

Character

Chase's vision narrowed to that tiny fracture, his leaking O_2 tank suddenly minor compared to the threat of an immediate loss of pressure. The truck lurched forward and Chase rolled off into the dirt. When he hit the ground, the crack in his faceplate grew several centimeters in length. With Chase in a near-panic, his sight flew to his suit's pressure gauge. It was holding, but his air was almost gone.

Acting purely on instinct, he brought the rifle to his shoulder, forced his focus past his cracked faceplate, and squeezed the trigger. His target was a vague shape through a swirling cloud of dust. Two rounds. Three. The truck continued.

The O_2 alarm sounding in his ear fragmented his concentration. He forced it out of his mind and squeezed the trigger again.

The left side of the truck sagged as a bullet ripped through the rear tire. The dust screen thickened as the wheel began to drag.

Chase shifted his aim to the other side and fired again. The right rear popped three shots later and the truck ground to a halt.

Character viewpoint (what he is going through)

This example illustrates the difference between a scene that's about the action and a scene that's about the character. The original version tells you what's happening in the story. The revised passage emphasizes character viewpoint. It shows you what Chase is going through.

Notice also that everything Chase does makes his situation worse. He rolls off the truck and the crack in his faceplate grows. When he shoots a tire to slow the truck, the dust screen thickens, making his target harder to see. The passage ends as soon as the truck stops, but in the book, the villain climbs out and shoots back at Chase, who has no cover. Each of these developments increases tension.

Here's another example. Remember the whizzing-bullet hook? The following passage takes place a few paragraphs later, as the heroes try to evade the enemy. An early draft read:

> Two men in EVA suits came flying over the ridge, armed with automatic rifles and each riding a four-wheeled all-terrain cycle. They landed several meters out from the lip of the ridge, producing a cloud of fine gray dust around them.

When you describe something that threatens your characters, make it seem scary. A critiquer told me to dramatize the cycles' power, menace, and dangers. She advised me to make them loud, but sound doesn't travel through the vacuum of space. Chase, the viewpoint character, can't hear the powerful machines. Therefore, I can't use noise to make them frightening. Instead, I made their silence ominous:

> Then a pair of four-wheeled, all-terrain cycles flew over the ridge behind them, carrying men in pressure suits, armed with automatic rifles. **The machines had the air of grizzled beasts, predators on the trail of frightened prey. The distance they covered in their graceful flight was tale enough of the power and speed they possessed. And the complete, eerie silence produced by the intervening void only added to their hunter's image.**

In another example from later in the same scene, Chase's truck has crashed and the cycles are approaching. The lives of the good guys depend on whether the truck starts. Here's the early draft:

> Chase pulled himself into the driver's seat, restarted the transport, and pulled away. *Too easy*

Yawn! Never make anything easy. How about:

Chase pulled himself into the driver's seat and tried the ignition.

The transport was dead.

Already it's better. You can feel the tension that's lacking in the original version. The revised passage goes on:

Several rounds swept the compartment before Mike returned fire. When he did, the rider rolled off his bike and took cover behind it. Clark and Gloria joined the offensive. Cordova moved behind Chase and fired out the driver's window, forcing the second rider to take cover as well.

Chase turned up the O_2 bleed and tried the starter again. The motor roared once and died. More O_2. **He cranked up the fuel intake as well.** The transport came to life and he pulled away.

This version makes the reader believe, if only for a few paragraphs, that the truck's not going to start. It builds tension.

This single change may make the difference between this scene working or not working for the story, but not because of the tension it adds. Remember, Chase is the hero. If the truck starts right up, anybody in it can take the wheel. In the rewrite, Chase must do things that somebody less knowledgeable, or less cool-headed, might not have thought to do. He, and he alone, has the wherewithal to save the team.

Later, I come back to the hunter's image of the cycles for the end-of-scene hook. As soon as Chase and his team defeat the riders, a truckload of enemies rounds the corner:

The riders weren't hunters after all. They were merely dogs, sent to force the hunted up a tree and prevent it from fleeing before the hunters could arrive.

Chase set the scope aside. His lame vehicle was capable of only half the speed it had done before the collision. The dogs, it seemed, had succeeded.

Revealing Setting

Pay particular attention to how you've portrayed your setting. It must be:

1. realistic
2. memorable
3. not overly described
4. not described all at once
5. described as seen by the viewpoint character

If it's not, revise your description. Go back to your setting card. Have you made the impression you intended to make? If not, select different details or change the way your viewpoint character interprets the details. If you've given too many details, cut some out. Let the reader fill in the blanks. If you stopped the action to describe your setting, review "Enhancing Setting," Chapter 6, and "Information Dumps: Setting Description" in Chapter 8.

Make sure you've described your setting in a way that reveals the viewpoint character's attitude and emotional state. Is the room cramped, or cozy? Is it cluttered, or lived in? Are the furnishings antiques, or are they just old and outdated?

When Chase approaches the *Phoenix* crash site, he has time to take in the details that are important to his case:

Chase's first view of the **Phoenix** was a mere glint of sunlight on the horizon. As he drew closer, the fuselage came into view, jutting skyward from the flat terrain like a solitary tombstone in a garden of glittering metal. The effect gave a surreal beauty to the desolate scene.

The pod came to a stop at the boundary of the debris field. The ship was close now. The fuselage, largely intact, rested at an odd angle at the end of a long scar in the landscape. A debris field stretched out to the northwest, away from Chase's vehicle and the direction of the rover tracks. Dents and cracks that marred the hull suggested that the ship had tumbled into its final resting place. The aft section, the cargo hold, was mangled.

Chase not only notices the details but also assesses what they tell him about the crash. Contrast this with the following passage, which takes place during a gunfight inside the enemy stronghold:

> Two terrorists moved before them as they wound their way through the labyrinthine passages ...
>
> The defenders stopped at each intersection to fire a few odd rounds, which slowed Chase and his party, but the men never stayed in one place for long. Twice the terrorists fired through a window to bring down isolation doors and seal off part of the complex.
>
> "They're running out of ammo," Mike concluded.
>
> "They're herding us."

Here you get only a vague sense of passages, windows, and pressure doors. I left out the details because Chase doesn't have time to notice them.

Point of View

Make sure your scenes don't express something the viewpoint character wouldn't know, like what's happening someplace else or the cause of a phenomenon he doesn't understand. Don't express the thoughts, emotions, or motivations of other characters, except as they are interpreted by your viewpoint character.

Viewpoint violations can be subtle. See if you can spot the viewpoint violations in this excerpt from a critique submission. The scene is written from Tridia's point of view. J'Lel is *not* one of the prisoners.

> "What would you have us do with your captives, Ma'am?" Captain Heilen asked.
>
> Tridia still didn't glance at the men before she answered, but kept her eyes locked with J'Lel's.
>
> "Captain, is there a penalty for retaliating on a Challenge?"
>
> "Yes, Ma'am, as you know."

"What is that penalty?"

"Loss of two ranks, fifty lashes across the back, and six months in hard labor servitude."

The male captives began to look guilty and as fearful as the yellow-clad girl.

"And Captain, is there a penalty for the threat of retaliation made before witnesses?"

"Yes ... Commander." He faltered as he answered.

"And what is that penalty?"

Captain Heilen hesitated, glancing at the prisoners. Tridia knew one of them meant a great deal to him. She read it in his mind. "The penalty is ..."

Did you catch the viewpoint violations?

The male captives began to look guilty and as fearful as the yellow-clad girl.

Captain Heilen hesitated, glancing at the prisoners.

Because Tridia never took her eyes off J'Lel, she couldn't have known what the captives' expressions looked like or that Captain Heilen glanced at the prisoners. I would delete the first sentence entirely and the last clause of the second.

As a counterexample, the author could have inappropriately worded the final paragraph like this:

One of them meant a great deal to him. "The penalty is..."

If she had, the sentence in bold text would have also been a viewpoint violation. But because Tridia is a telepath, and because the author establishes in the original passage how Tridia knows what Captain Heilen is feeling, his fondness for the prisoner is shown firmly from Tridia's point of view.

Purge the viewpoint violations from your scenes.

Character Consistency

Look for inconsistencies in your characters. The following excerpts are from a critique submission.

The first-person viewpoint character, Clara, discovers the same stranger in two candid photos that she took at two separate sightseeing locations:

> The back of my neck tingled the way it always did when something strange happened.

Throughout the story, Clara experiences several events she finds strange, yet she never again experiences this back-of-her-neck tingling.

Later, Clara visits the home of a new acquaintance:

> I ... began browsing his floor-to-ceiling teak bookshelves — always a preferred pastime of mine.

Yet when she's in a library, filled with ancient texts potentially important to her research, Clara fails to peruse the shelves.

Tidbits like these often feel like good characterization when they first go onto the page, and spur-of-the-moment thoughts can generate ideas for character traits and quirks. You must go back through your manuscript, however, and pick out the ideas you want to keep. Make them consistent with other aspects of the character and consistent throughout the manuscript. Purge the rest.

Note any character changes on the character's profile (Chapter 2) so you'll remember them. If you don't catch the inconsistencies, your readers will.

Character Descriptions

Similar to setting, your character descriptions must be realistic, memorable, not overly described, and not described all at once. In addition, they must be described through action, in a manner that will evoke an emotional response on the part of the reader.

In *Venus Rain*, Professor Dennis La Roche is an old man, but to simply say, "La Roche was old" would not evoke an emotion from the reader. Consider this introduction instead:

> "... on this thirtieth anniversary of the Venus terraforming project." Professor La Roche spoke from the stage, hunched like an invalid over the podium. His voice, raspy with age, carried through the speakers to every corner of the room.

This passage imparts a sense of fragility not offered by simple description.

In an earlier reference, I have shown La Roche to be respected and liked by at least one other main character. Introducing him as a hunched invalid helps generate sympathy on the part of the reader, especially when I introduce the villain, Colonel Chang, a few paragraphs later.

Chang interrupts La Roche's speech and orders a crony to execute one of La Roche's colleagues, which the crony does. Then:

> As [Chang] stepped up to the microphone, the spotlight revealed a grotesque visage, red and raw across the man's forehead, the right side of his nose, and most of his cheek and jaw. Skin flaked from his face, as though it had been scorched by the Mercury sun and had only begun to heal. "Now I have your attention," he said in accented English. "I am Colonel Chang Chaozong." He held his right forearm level, with his fingers slightly cupped. His wrist rotated back and forth as though driven by an oscillating servo. "I claim this station for the People's Republic of China. Each of you will live or die by my command."

Would a simple description of flaking skin and a nervous wrist have made him quite so intimidating?

Introducing Characters

Worlds Asunder includes a scene in which Victoria Powers, the President of the United States, meets with Chief of Staff Warren Parker, Secretary of State Anthony Mariano, CIA Director Tom O'Leary, Political Adviser Anne Portman, Secretary of State Dan Norton, several military experts and analysts, and a delegation from the European Union, including European Secretary of State Andrew Yates, the EU Ambassador to the United States, and half a dozen representatives from the EU military and intelligence communities, including a man named Wolfgang Das. *Whew!* That's about twenty new characters. How can I help the reader keep them straight?

1   Limit ways of referencing newly introduced characters.

Pick one way to reference each character and stick with it. Let's take Anthony Mariano, for example. Suppose I introduced him with his full name and title, then called him Anthony, then Tony, then Mariano, then the state secretary. Now, instead of one appellation, I've given him five. If I do this with all twenty characters, I'll give the reader a hundred new names to remember. All in the same scene!

2   Don't introduce unimportant characters by name.

In the scene described above, I've given names only to Powers, Parker, Norton, Mariano, Portman, O'Leary, Yates, and Das. The remaining characters are unimportant. They exist only to fill the seats, to make the meeting large enough to be credible. Though some of the unnamed characters speak, my decision not to name them signals the reader that they're unimportant. He won't try to catalog them along with the named characters.

Still, remembering eight new characters is a lot to expect of your reader.

3   Don't introduce too many characters at once.

If you must introduce several characters in a single

scene, don't introduce them all at once. Think back to a party at which you were introduced to a dozen people at the same time. Did you remember all their names ten minutes later? If you do this to your reader, he'll have the same difficulty.

Now remember a time when you arrived at a party early and the other guests trickled in later. You met one or two at a time and chatted with each for a few minutes before being introduced to the next. Did this help you remember them?

In *Worlds Asunder*, I delayed the introduction of the European characters until the President's second meeting, which takes place in a separate scene. Doing so dropped two named characters, Yates and Das, from the original introductions.

I begin my scene with President Powers in the Oval Office. As the most important character in the scene, I introduce her first, alone, so the reader will remember her. When Warren Parker arrives, the two trade a few lines of dialogue to give the reader a chance to get to know him before Dan Norton and a contingent of unnamed experts and analysts show up. The scene includes a short discussion with him before they all move to the Situation Room, where I introduce the remaining three characters.

This is a powerful technique. Add character identifiers (lines, mannerisms, and props) and a few well-placed reminders of which character holds which office. Now your reader will keep up.

Additional Resource

If you need additional help banging your scenes into shape, I recommend *Novelist's Essential Guide to Crafting Scenes*, by Raymond Obstfeld. This excellent reference covers every facet of scene structure and content. It also gives specific guidance for several types of scenes (such as action, romantic, comic, and final scenes) that are beyond the scope of *Revising Fiction*.

Exercises

1   Select a scene you've written. Write three separate beginnings for the scene. First, introduce an interesting
character who wants something simple, and then provide a minor obstacle. Do this in one or two paragraphs.
Second, make the first sentence an intriguing line of
dialogue. Continue the conversation without backtrack-
ing to set up context. Third, devise the most intense
beginning you can justify, given the intensity of the rest
of the scene. Which of these hooks works best for this
scene?

2   Read through a scene you've written. Have you used the
name of an emotion anywhere in the text? If so, rewrite
the passage to show the emotion without using its name
or a synonym.

3   Select a scene in which you've introduced at least four
characters, preferably six or more. Using the following
techniques, revise the scene to help the reader keep the
characters straight: use action to describe them, rather
than writing static descriptions. Refer to each in only
one way. Remove the names of unimportant characters.
Introduce the characters one or two at a time. Add identifying lines, props, or mannerisms for each character.
Have someone read both versions of the scene. Ask the
reader which he liked better and why.

4   Select a scene you've written. Write three separate endings for the scene. First, end with a cliffhanger. Put a
character into trouble and leave her there. Second, end
with revealing internal monologue. Show something
surprising about the character that the reader didn't

already know. Third, use emotional dialogue to reveal some aspect of one of your characters. Which of these endings works best with the scene?

5   Select an action scene you've written that seems (to you or to someone else) to lack the intended emotional impact. Put yourself in the place of the viewpoint character and rewrite the scene. Don't focus on the events that are happening. Focus, instead, on what the viewpoint character experiences as a result of the events. Don't make anything easy. Build tension at every opportunity. Have someone read both versions of the scene. Ask the reader which she liked better and why.

Read carefully (handwritten)

10

Case Studies

So far, I've discussed how to correct one problem at a time, and that's how you should correct them. Nevertheless, it's instructive to look at the self-editing process for longer passages and passages that exhibit multiple problems, to see how revision can transform them.

Case Study 1

The following excerpt is from the opening scene of an early-draft critique submission:

Tama-pov (handwritten)

Beginning is strong (handwritten)

"Hey, Tama Fook, did you see that?" he asked as he crouched down, "frack, what is that?"

"Quiet Greggis!"

"But that black mist just came out of the ground." The two saw part of the black mist rise up, the top part of the mist looked like it was looking around. To Tama Fook it looked like it was moving on its own. He knew this was some kind of sentient being. This was something that they didn't want to meddle with right now. Whatever this thing was, they wanted nothing to do with it. *He / POV* (handwritten)

Conflict (good) (handwritten)

"Silence. We don't want it to come over here. Whatever it is."

Greggis whispered, "It's moving and there's no wind. What do we do?" horror started to mask over Tama Fook's otherwise happy face. *Tell* (handwritten) *masked* (handwritten)

[handwritten margin notes: "what are they", "we", "they", "satchels", "buried Someplace"]

"Yes I know it's moving. We need to be quiet!" Tama Fook whispered, and then he hit his brother on the arm.

They crouched down behind a rock as they watched the mist move to the northwest. This thing, whatever it was, they watched it moving really slow and they couldn't figure out what it was. Or why it moved on its own.

Should we follow it? Or should we go tell somebody what we saw?" Greggis said.

"Well, I'm not following it, Greggis. And I'm not going back to Dusa City without the satchels."

[handwritten margin note: "#1" with bracket, "INFO DUMP"]

Tama Fook and Greggis were brothers that roamed all over Saorsa looking for precious stones and valuable metals for the young King Ertas. Their parents were killed years ago by a Skolkor's Garb Army when the Garbs sacked Sarak. They had survived only by being in a small nurturing room in the rear of their parents lodge. An elderly lady had found them when she heard them screaming because they were hungry. They knew nothing of what had happened to their city, they were told by this elderly lady the events that took place. They grew up on the streets of Dusa City, they stole what they needed to survive and they killed only when it was desperately necessary. The lady that had found them moved them to Dusa City and she died six years later of a skin disease. The two brothers grew up alone and in their late teens Ertas took over Dusa City as the new king. They were happy that the city was changing for the better.

[handwritten margin note: "#2"]

It was only three months ago that they had taken this job as King Ertas' jewel searchers, they had found some just outside of Dusa City and they found more the farther they traveled into the Dry Lands. When they filled a satchel to the point that they could barely carry it, they would [bury it]. And make a map of where they had put it in the ground. They had found more nuggets of precious metals than stones and that was what the new King wanted. They were going to turn back a day ago and bring all of the satchels to the castle but they wanted to fill two more satchels before they left the Dry Lands. They had seen the black footprints before but they knew nothing of what they were. They were a hundred yards away when Greggis saw the black mist coming about the ground.

This excerpt has a lot to offer. According to the characters' backstory, they walk the gray line between good and evil, even killing when necessary. Walking this line always makes a character more interesting. From a story-line standpoint, the beginning is strong. The author throws his characters right into the conflict, pitting them against an ominous being they don't understand.

Beyond that, however, the passage suffers from nearly every problem described in this book. It contains information dumps. It's rife with *tell*, it lacks emotional intensity, and it needs more fully developed setting and character descriptions. It has problems related to prose and dialogue (discussed in Chapters 11 and 12) as well as poor spelling, grammar, punctuation, and word usage. In other words, it's exactly what I expect a first draft to be.

If your first drafts look like this, you're not alone. Mine exhibit all these problems, often to a greater extent than the passage above. My point: You can fix anything through revision and it's worth the effort to do so. Let's see how it works.

1 Information dumps

This excerpt isn't a complete scene, let alone a chapter or manuscript. Therefore, it's difficult to evaluate it for most of the problems discussed in Chapters 1 through 8. We can, however, look for information dumps, which we find in the last two paragraphs. These paragraphs are problematic for several reasons. First, they stop the action. The author has pulled his reader away from the conflict for a historical sidebar.

Second, the paragraphs destroy the suspense the author establishes in the preceding sentence:

"And I'm not going back to Dusa City without the satchels."

This line provides the first hint about who these characters are and what they're up to. The satchels aren't much for the reader to go on, but that's part of the reason they build suspense. Obviously, they're important, so they must contain something of value.

The characters don't have the satchels in their possession. This gives them an immediate goal. They may need to embark on a long quest to recover them, or they may just have to walk ten feet and pick them up. We don't know at this point. But this single line of dialogue makes it clear that the mist constitutes a danger in retrieving them and that at least one character is resolved to brave that risk.

All this entices the reader to forge ahead, to find answers to questions like: Who are these guys? Why are they here? What do the satchels contain? Why are they important? The author then sidetracks into a passage of backstory that answers these questions without an exploratory process.

Finally, the paragraphs provide information that seems unimportant at the moment. They present meaningful details in the characters' histories, but they're not relevant to the events immediately transpiring. The viewpoint character has no reason to ponder them at that moment.

Therefore, these two paragraphs must be cut. The information in them may be revealed elsewhere in the manuscript.

In the rest of this case study, I'll step through the sections of Chapter 9 and correct the scene problems, one at a time. You may be surprised by the result.

2   Scene structure

Though this isn't a complete scene, we can study the elements the author has introduced so far:

- Hook: I'll discuss the hook in the section on scene opening below.
- Goal: The characters want to get their satchels and get back to Dusa City.
- Obstacle: The black mist.
- Action to overcome the obstacle: The characters' immediate reaction is to hide, but the mist comes at them anyway. Because the excerpt ends here, we don't know how the rest of the scene plays out.
- Reaction: Whatever the mist will do.
- Problem leading into the next scene: The actions of the mist will likely lead to a hook at the end of the scene.

From a structure standpoint, this is a healthy scene.

3 Scene opening

I like the hook provided by the opening paragraph:

> "Hey Tama Fook, did you see that?" he asked as he crouched down, "frack, what is that?"

Having a character ask the questions, "Did you see that?" and "What is that?" makes the reader want to know what the character sees. Right away something interesting is happening. This provides the hook.

The writing in this paragraph can be tightened, though, and the reader should know who "he" is. I'll discuss ways to resolve these problems in Chapters 11 and 12 and then return to this scene for Case Study 4 in Chapter 13.

4 Show and tell

This scene contains a lot of telling dialogue, but I'll let that slide until we get to "Informative Dialogue" in Chapter 12. Here, I'll address the non-dialogue passages of *tell*:

> ... the top part of the mist looked like it was looking around. To Tama Fook it looked like it was moving on its own. He knew this was some kind of evil sentient being.

Here, the author tells the reader that the mist is moving on its own, that it is evil, and that it's sentient. Instead, he should show her what the mist does and let her draw these conclusions for herself. Here's one way to do that:

> Still as the dead, the air contained not a breath of wind. Nonetheless, the mist moved. Aimlessly at first, then it turned toward the brothers and the air grew cold.

This passage gives the reader only the observable facts: the mist moves in the absence of wind, it turns and approaches, and the air grows cold. The reader can now deduce all the things the author concluded for her in the initial passage. I've worked in a couple of setting details along the way: a lack of wind and the implication of an otherwise-warm temperature.

Here's another passage of *tell*:

> This was something that they didn't want to meddle with right now. Whatever this thing was, they wanted nothing to do with it.

These sentences tell what the next sentence shows:

> "Silence, we don't want it to come over here. Whatever it is."

Because the author shows in the dialogue what he told in the narrative, the revision is simple: delete the sentences that tell and leave the one that shows. Furthermore, the author doesn't need the whole dialogue line to show this. He can say it all with one word:

"Silence."

Another case of *tell*:

They couldn't figure out what it was, or why it moved on its own.

The author can delete this sentence. His earlier description of the mist makes it clear that Greggis and Tama Fook don't understand it.

5   Revealing setting

In the first page-and-a-half of Chapter 1, the setting consists of ground (the mist came out of it), a lack of wind (stated by Greggis), a rock (that the characters crouched behind), and a city somewhere named Dusa City. That's it. The last two paragraphs of the original submission contain additional details, but these are backstory, not immediate setting.

The author must provide something that gives the reader a picture of the characters' setting. Is it lush or barren? Hot or cold? Deserted or populated? Noisy or quiet? Is there anything around them (structures, terrain features, animals, or equipment)? Are there any smells?

He mustn't stop the action with a long, narrative description. Instead, he must work the details, little by little, into the action of the story, wherever the opportunity presents itself. I'll point out when I do this, here and in Chapter 13.

6 Point of view

It's difficult to determine who the viewpoint character is in this scene. At first, I assumed it was Greggis because he's the first speaking character. Yet later the passage says:

> To Tama Fook it looked like it was moving on its own.

This line is written from Tama Fook's point of view, because Greggis can't know what Tama Fook thinks. Then we find:

> Horror started to mask over Tama Fook's otherwise happy face.

Tama Fook can't see his own face, so this line is written from Greggis's viewpoint.

Point of view is particularly clouded in the third paragraph, which states:

> **The two saw** the black mist rise up ... **They wanted** nothing to do with it.

The author must decide who his viewpoint character is. He can then strengthen point of view by revealing the thoughts and emotions of the viewpoint character, and by showing the physical description, gestures, and expressions of the other character.

For the sake of this case study, I selected Tama Fook as the viewpoint character. The opening could read:

> Tama Fook and his brother, Greggis, crouched behind a large granite boulder jutting from the dry earth.

This sentence helps establish viewpoint by naming Tama Fook first. It also reveals a bit of setting in the opening sentence. Notice the specificity: not just a boulder, but a granite boulder; not just earth, but dry earth.

Because this sentence repeats the original reference to crouching, the original should be removed:

> "Hey, Tama Fook, did you see that? Frack. What is that?"

7 Character description

As with the setting, this passage contains little physical description of the characters. What do Greggis and Tama Fook look like? Do they have any identifying physical traits or mannerisms that might be revealed within the context of this scene?

Correct this problem by inserting bits of descriptive action as opportunities arise. For example, I like this line:

> Horror started to mask over Tama Fook's otherwise happy face.

Because I've decided to write the scene from Tama Fook's point of view, and because he can't see his own face, I can preserve this line only by moving the expression to Greggis's face. While I'm at it, I'll take the opportunity to include some description:

> Weeks of beard clung to Greggis's face in ragged, dust-clotted knots. Horror began to mask his expression.

I omitted the reference to his "otherwise happy face" for two reasons. This was originally a reference to Tama Fook. Greggis's face might not be "otherwise happy," as Tama Fook's is. Also, it's better to show this rather than tell it. The author should portray Tama Fook as a happy character throughout the story rather than stating it on the first page.

8 Putting it all together

Read the passage with the changes discussed above and a few corrections to punctuation:

> Tama Fook and his brother, Greggis, crouched behind a large granite boulder jutting from the dry earth.
>
> "Hey, Tama Fook, did you see that? Frack. What is that?"
>
> "Quiet, Greggis!"
>
> "But that black mist just came out of the ground." Tama Fook saw part of the black mist rise up. Still as the dead, the air contained not a breath of wind. Nonetheless, the mist moved. Aimlessly at first, then it turned toward the brothers and the air grew cold.
>
> "Silence."
>
> Weeks of beard clung to Greggis's face in ragged, dust-clotted knots. Horror began to mask his expression. "It's moving and there's no wind. What do we do?"
>
> "Yes. I know it's moving. We need to be quiet!" Tama Fook whispered, and then he hit his brother on the arm.
>
> They crouched down behind a rock as they watched the mist move to the northwest, this thing, whatever it was, they watched it moving really slow.
>
> "Should we follow it? Or should we go tell somebody what we saw?"
>
> "Well, I'm not following it, Greggis. And I'm not going back to Dusa City without the satchels."

These changes improve the passage significantly, yet it still needs a fair amount of work. The remaining problems involve prose and dialogue. I'll discuss these topics in great detail in the next two chapters, then revisit this scene in Chapter 13 to address the remaining problems.

Case Study 2

Read the following excerpt from a critique submission in which Tridia, a telepath, has just come through a crowded spaceport after a grueling physical challenge. The passage suffers from one principal scene-related problem. Can you identify it?

Tridia had private rooms on an upper level at the far end of the dormitory building, where the cradle delivered her to within a few feet of her door. She struggled from the cradle, barely able to stand. Dealing with that many minds at once when she was on the verge of mental and physical exhaustion had drained her energy reserves. Her door swam before her eyes and she stumbled. Adrenaline rushed through her system. This couldn't happen, shouldn't happen. Even at her most exhausted she could maintain her balance. If her enemies found her in this condition they would show no mercy. In slow motion she made her way to the three-inch thick turanium door that opened only to her voice, palm, and retina-prints in combination. She possessed one of the most secure entrances on the entire planet, but she feared the security would work against her this time.

Tridia sensed another mind nearby as she positioned herself to unlock the door. Aggressive and intense thoughts slammed into her brain causing excruciating pain. The person counted on 'the gas' to make her unaware of the weapon pointing at her back. The weapon would fire once the lock released. Beyond that, vulgar images mingled with her pain and she winced in an attempt to clear her mind. She looked at the wall behind her. The person had concealed the weapon too well for her to find it quickly.

Tridia knew she couldn't battle in this condition nor could she escape down the hall or back into the tube. Her only hope lay in getting inside her room.

She made herself concentrate. The retinal scanner guaranteed her position in a specific place when the lock sprang, which indicated the weapon's target area. So, she reasoned, something attached to the door would send a signal to the weapon. It required precious moments to locate the tiny object straddling the crevice between the door and the frame. The simple device worked on fluid balance. Any micron of movement and it would trigger the weapon. Her fuzzy thoughts fought all efforts at organization but she sensed the predator inching closer. He waited for something. Perhaps the firing of the weapon? If so, she had a few extra heartbeats to think.

Tridia leaned heavily against her door. She had to stay out of range of the weapon and still open the door. The weapon would fire at the retinal scanner when the object moved. Then it dawned on her, she could be elsewhere when the weapon fired. Taking the fake surveillance disk from her pocket again she slid across the door and as far away from the scanner as she could, then used the disk to dislodge the device. A wide stun beam caught Tridia's right arm at the elbow when the weapon fired. She dropped the disk from her numbed hand. With disregard for her injury she moved to the scanner, used her left hand to lift the right palm against the biometric reader, and spoke her code as clearly as she could. For one frozen heartbeat she feared the lock wouldn't recognize her slurred voice, then she heard it click as the door swung outward. She slipped inside and shut the door just as hurried footsteps rounded the corner.

Tridia forced herself to take deep breaths of untainted air as she crossed the room, putting distance between herself and the door.

Did you spot the problem? What is it? If you said, "There's no tension," you're right. This case study focuses on injecting tension into a scene.

The way it's written, this scene is about the events rather than about Tridia and what she's experiencing. The reader feels detached, as though observing the events from a distance. Instead, she should experience the scene as though she *is* Tridia. Do this by emphasizing Tridia's problems, *as Tridia perceives them,* at every opportunity.

Here's one way the scene may be rewritten with greater tension while preserving as much of the author's original wording as possible. At the end of the passage, I'll discuss the changes that I made and why.

> Tridia had private rooms on an upper level at the far end of the dormitory building. The cradle delivered her to within a few feet of her door. She struggled from the cradle, barely able to stand. Dealing with that many minds at once when she was on the verge of mental and physical exhaustion had drained her reserves. Her door swam before her eyes and she stumbled.
>
> She sensed another mind nearby, a man — she was sure of the gender — his thoughts infused with violent intent. The intensity of his emotions slammed into her brain. She clenched her lip between her teeth to keep from crying out in pain.
>
> Adrenaline rushed through her system, but her movements were too slow to meet the extremity of her need. She was too far gone to survive a fight now, and it was too late to climb back into the cradle, which had already departed to serve another customer. Her only hope was to get into her room. But she had one of the most secure dormitories on the planet, with a three-inch thick turanium door that opened only to her voice, palm, and retina-prints in combination. She'd never gain entry in time.

She stepped up to the retinal scanner and forced herself to concentrate. The images invading her mind began to fragment. Shards of thought separated from the tumult of vulgar images that mingled with her pain. Small though the fragments were, she analyzed them: a transparent gas, a hidden weapon, and one that surprised her. Patience.

The assailant was waiting for something, perhaps the springing of a trap. She had a few more heartbeats to think, but the gas flooded into her bloodstream and her mind began to succumb to darkness.

She forced her eye open with her thumb and finger so the scanner could see her retina. Then she saw it, a minute radio trigger mounted near the electronic eye of the scanner. The sensor, which was based on fluid balance, would detect even the slightest movement in the door and ... what?

Think. There must be a weapon concealed in the synthetic ferns that decorated the corridor behind her, but she didn't have time to find it. Her faculties and the patience of the enemy were fading.

She whipped the false surveillance disk from her pocket, launched it at the trigger and sprang away, but the stun from the concealed weapon was set to wide field and her right arm went numb and useless from the elbow down.

The assailant rushed her. She pretended not to notice until she could hear his breath at her ear, then she ducked, took his weight on her hips and rocked with it. The force of his charge carried him over her to sprawl with a grunt onto the floor.

With her left hand, Tridia forced her right palm onto the biometric reader and slurred her code into the microphone.

Nothing. The door remained closed as the attacker climbed to his feet and drew a stun pistol, his face concealed by the gas filter he breathed through.

Gas and stun clouded Tridia's perception and thickened her tongue. She spoke her code again, forcing herself to enunciate each syllable.

The door clicked open and the assailant fired.

Tridia's instincts carried her inside just as the stun beam swept the corridor. She pressed the door closed, sealed herself in safety, and gulped down lungfuls of untainted air until most of her senses returned.

In this passage, I've corrected only the scene-level problems. I haven't polished the prose, which would raise the tension higher. Let's look at the specific changes.

1   I took out the following sentences:

> This couldn't happen, shouldn't happen. Even at her most exhausted she could maintain her balance. If her enemies found her in this condition they would show no mercy.

These lines ponder what might happen if Tridia's enemies appeared at that moment. Instead, I moved up the statement, "Tridia sensed another mind nearby," and established the intruder's violent intent. Now the reader knows immediately that the enemy is there. Tridia no longer hypothesizes about a possible attack. The attack is happening. Without that, the scene opening fails to hook the reader.

2   Instead of telling the reader that the intensity of the emotions caused Tridia pain, I show it by describing her reaction to it:

> She clenched her lip between her teeth to keep from crying out in pain.

This reaction is specific to Tridia because she must hide the fact that she's a telepath. Because her telepathy is the cause of her pain, this shows the lengths to which she'll go in order to hide it.

3   Throughout the passage, I changed "the person" to "the attacker," "the assailant," "the enemy" — anything but "the person." "The person" is much too unemotional a reference to someone who represents a danger to the viewpoint character.

4   I clarified the author's reference to "the gas." Because she put the words in quotes, I assumed it was something she called "the gas" that was not really a gas. I actually thought I'd missed some earlier reference that would explain what "the gas" was. I realized it was real only after she mentioned the untainted air in Tridia's room. By that point the danger had passed and I no longer cared that the gas had been real.

5   I delayed the description of Tridia's security until it was obvious it was part of the problem. I changed "one of the most secure entrances" to "one of the most secure dormitories." I would hope Tridia's entire home is at least as secure as the entrance.

6   I changed "In slow motion" to "her movements were too slow to meet the extremity of her need." In the revised passage, Tridia is in genuine danger at this point in the narrative, so the author can make the statement stronger and more emotional.

7   I gave a reason why Tridia couldn't step back into the cradle.

8   Throughout the scene, particularly when Tridia finds the radio trigger and deduces the nature of the trap, I tried to make her assessment of the situation more

instinctive than analytical. She's emotionally and physically exhausted from the events of the previous scene, she's bombarded by painful images, she's been gassed, and an enemy is about to attack. She has neither the time nor the capacity for an analysis. What remains are her instincts and training.

9   I tried to make clear what Tridia gains through telepathy, what she knows through observation, and what she surmises through guesswork.

10   The author provided no description of the hallway, leaving the impression that it's bare, undecorated wall. Yet that would give the assailant no place to conceal a weapon. Not knowing what the corridor looks like, I created synthetic ferns as a hiding place. The author will have to describe her own vision of what this hallway looks like.

11   The disabling of the trap is the first point at which I changed the events of the scene. I didn't think Tridia's enemy would sit idle while she analyzed and defeated his trap, so I made her solution more expedient. She now throws the disk to dislodge the sensor rather than prying the sensor loose.

12   I had to wonder what the assailant was doing while Tridia was disarming the trap and getting away. In the revision, as soon as the weapon goes off, Tridia's enemy attacks her bodily to prevent her from gaining the safety of her room. I gave him a breathing device to explain why he would enter a hallway filled with harmful gas and to conceal his identity, which wasn't revealed in the original passage.

13 I ratcheted the tension higher by making Tridia's door fail to open on the first try and by having her enemy draw a gun.

14 I tightened the wording and made several references more specific:
- "Positioned herself to unlock the door" became "stepped up to the retinal scanner."
- The two references, "something attached to the door" and "the tiny object straddling the crevice between the door and the frame," combined to become, "radio trigger mounted near the electronic eye of the scanner."
- "… driven by a desire to capture her for some purpose" became "infused with violent intent."

15 Finally, notice the difference in paragraph length. The short paragraphs in the revised passage increase the pace of the action and help the reader feel the tension.

You may have noticed that this passage fails to provide an end-of-scene hook. That's okay. The end of the excerpted passage is not the end of the scene.

Part III

The Little Stuff

In the next three chapters, you'll narrow your focus from the larger-scope issues to the minutiae of the prose and dialogue. I call this part "the little stuff." That's not to say prose and dialogue are any less important than manuscript organization or scene structure. It's merely a recognition that words, sentences, and paragraphs are smaller than scenes, chapters, and manuscripts.

Your words and sentence structure are the nuts and bolts of your story, or rather the nails and lumber from which it's constructed. And like the nails and lumber that make up your house, if your words and sentences are done right, they don't show. When a guest visits your house, you want him to enjoy your home, not inspect the construction. Similarly, when a person reads your book, you want him to enjoy your story, not ponder your words and sentences.

11

Prose

There are many ways in which your word choices and sentence structure can weaken your writing style. I'll step through them the way you should look for them in your writing: one at a time. This approach can be tedious and time-consuming. If done right, polishing your prose will be the single most time-consuming step of the self-editing process. Nevertheless, the results are worth the effort. Your writing style will dramatically improve. The steps in this chapter will make bad writing good or good writing great. If you revise your manuscript to purge every problem discussed in this book, you can make terrible writing phenomenal.

Before you begin, save a copy of your current draft and continue working with a separate file. The next steps focus on making your writing efficient, clear, and effective. They can occasionally make it sound choppy, particularly at paragraph transitions. When you read each scene after editing your prose, you may decide to undo a few of the changes (but only a few) in order to smooth the rhythm of the text.

To-Be Verbs

The to-be verbs are: *am, is, are, was, were, be, been,* and *being.* Avoid these whenever possible. They can appear in a number of ways that weaken your writing style.

1 Passive voice

Passive voice refers to a sentence in which the object of the action is the subject of the sentence. For example:

> Sue was hit by Bill.
>
> Sue was hit.

You can eliminate passive voice by turning the sentence around so the person or thing doing the action becomes the subject of the sentence. This is called *active voice*.

> Bill hit Sue.

Passive voice is more wordy and less direct than active voice. It's more laborious to read and often harder to understand. Use it only when the object of the action is much more important than the subject, or when the subject is unknown:

> He was murdered.

2 Past progressive tense

Past progressive tense indicates ongoing action in the past:

> The smell was coming from the basement.

Change past progressive tense to past tense whenever possible:

> The smell came from the basement.

This makes the narrative more immediate, more compelling to read. It gives it more punch.

3 Statements of being

A statement of being tells the reader what something is without showing action. Statements of being are pure description. Learn to recognize them. Purge them from your style. For example:

Statement of being:	**Statement of action:**
• It was after two when the game started.	• The game started after two.
• Joan was there when it happened.	• Joan arrived before it happened.

The following excerpt, the opening paragraph of a non-fiction short story, is from a critique submission. Notice the profusion of to-be verbs.

It **was** dark both inside and outside the cabin of the Super Constellation. It **was** night and we **were** somewhere over the North Atlantic. The four huge propellers imparted a noise and vibration onto the airframe that wore on both crew and equipment. Behind me **were** a half dozen air controllers, their eyes focused on the radar screens in front of them. They **were** tracking each plane that crossed the Atlantic headed in the direction of the United States. They knew the schedule of the airlines, the typical speed and altitudes of airliners, transport planes and of Soviet bombers. Their job **was** to identify any plane that didn't belong there and had flight characteristics that might make it a potential enemy. My job as radioman **was** to transmit in Morse code their observations to our operational base in

Newfoundland. This **was** the cold war, and we **were** on radar patrol.

This paragraph contains nine to-be verbs, which are shown in bold text. Most are unnecessary:

> We flew at night, somewhere over the North Atlantic. The four huge propellers of the Super Constellation imparted a noise and vibration onto the airframe that wore on both crew and equipment. In the darkness behind me sat a half dozen air controllers with their eyes focused on their radar screens, tracking each plane that crossed the Atlantic toward the United States. They knew the schedule of the airlines, the typical speed and altitudes of airliners, transport planes and of Soviet bombers. They must identify any plane that didn't belong there and had flight characteristics that marked it as a potential enemy. As a radioman, I transmitted their observations in Morse code to our operational base in Newfoundland.
>
> This **was** the cold war, and we **were** on radar patrol.

This revision eliminates all but two to-be verbs. I moved the last sentence into a separate paragraph for emphasis. The difference between the first passage and the second is subtle but important. Because to-be verbs don't indicate action, at best they create a static image in the reader's mind. They don't evoke emotion. A story that relies upon to-be verbs will fail to hold the reader's attention no matter how interesting the topic.

That said, you can't expect to eliminate all to-be verbs from your writing, especially from dialogue. Nevertheless, purge as many as possible.

Search your manuscript electronically for the words *am, is, are, was, were, be, been,* and *being.* Use the Find/Replace function of your word processor to change the text format of these words to a different color (say, blue). Doing so will help you find them during editing. Once you've finished revising, Select All and change the text back to black.

As-ing Sentence Structures

Minimize "as" or "-ing" sentence structures that put action in subordinate clause. Consider this sentence:

Collect**ing** her things, Ginny ran inside.

This type of phrasing can lead you to describe physical impossibilities. Here it suggests that Ginny collected her things *while* she was running. I meant that she collected her things first, then ran inside. Therefore, I should have written:

Ginny collected her things and ran inside.

Another harmful form of the as-ing structure is the combined beat and attributive. A beat is an action performed by a character to identify her as the speaker of a line of dialogue. An attributive is a phrase, like "he said" or "she said," that identifies the speaker. Consider the following:

"I'm going out," she said, snatch**ing** her coat from the closet.

"She said" is an attributive. "Snatching her coat from the closet" is a beat. You never need both. Fortunately, this problem is easy to fix. Wherever you find it, delete the attributive:

"I'm going out." She snatched her coat from the closet.

As-ing sentences are not necessarily bad as long as they don't suffer from either of these problems. Furthermore, you want to use a variety of sentence structures in your writing. Be aware, however, that putting action into a subordinate clause can make it seem incidental, as though tacked on as an afterthought. As such, don't use the as-ing structure profusely.

'led viewpoint intruders, are words like *saw,*
that take the reader out of the character's
following example from an early draft of
…nder is the viewpoint character:

er **watched** the controller take his seat.

The word "watched" distances the reader from Snider. The reader is no longer in Snider's head. She's standing back, watching Snider as Snider watches the action. I revised the passage to say:

The controller took his seat.

Now the reader stays in Snider's head and experiences the action from there.

Consider this example from a critique submission, in which the filter words are shown in bold text. "I" refers to a woman named Clara.

I **looked** around at my fellow passengers. I **overheard** snatches of conversation in Italian. I **saw** parents feeding snacks to children, even a breast-feeding mother.

Here, the reader isn't looking at passengers, overhearing conversations, or seeing parents feed children. The reader watches Clara as Clara looks at, overhears, and sees the action of the scene. These words have become a filter between Clara and the reader.

The author can eliminate the first sentence because Clara doesn't see herself looking around. The rest of the passage can be written without filter words:

All around me, people spoke in Italian. Parents fed snacks to their children. One woman nursed her infant.

In this passage, the reader becomes Clara and experiences the action firsthand.

Other words, like *looking* and *turning* — anything that indicates eye movement without expressing emotion — can have the same effect as filter words. This is shown in the next example, from another critique submission:

"Just do it." Digger **watched** the Field of Bones. His eyes shone dimly with the pale glow of the Sight as he **stared** north past the islands of tilted wooden stakes marking the commoners graves. Beyond hung a legion of paper lanterns, burned out for hours now, under which the paupers' children lay silent. He **searched** the darkness at the foot of Watchers Hill, then **shifted** his vision upwards along the tumble of its rocky slopes. Ancient mausoleums loomed on the crest. The shadows there, bloated and heavy, held fast to stone and vine, but Digger had the Sight and nothing moved yet in those depths. And nothing would, if the diversionary fires on the other side of the hill held out until dawn.

Filler words

This scene is written from Digger's point of view. The reader should see the setting through his eyes. Eliminate the filter words and the reader becomes Digger:

"Just do it." Digger's sight illuminated the Field of Bones in ways that he could see, even in the darkest part of the night. North, beyond islands of tilted wooden stakes that marked the commoners graves, hung a legion of burned out paper lanterns, under which the paupers' children lay silent. Ancient mausoleums loomed atop the tumble of rocky slopes that fronted Watchers Hill. The shadows there, bloated and heavy, held fast to stone and vine, but the sight penetrated even those. Nothing moved yet in their depths. And nothing would, if the diversionary fires on the other side of the hill held out until dawn.

Thinker Attributives

A thinker attributive is similar to a dialogue attributive (discussed in Chapter 12). It uses phrases like he *thought*, or *knew*, or *remembered* to show what your character is thinking. Don't rely on these devices. You're writing from the character's point of view; therefore, any thoughts you express are assumed to be the thoughts of the character. This makes thinker attributives unnecessary. In fact, thinker attributives are just another kind of filter word.

Look at the following example from a critique submission:

> He seems nice enough, she **thought**, but he must be a weirdo because no one really runs around with green hair and wears a tuxedo jacket over coveralls.

Without the thinker attributive, this becomes:

> He seemed nice enough, but he must have been a weirdo because no one really runs around with green hair and wears a tuxedo jacket over coveralls.

Alternatively, the author can eliminate both the thinker attributive and the to-be verb:

> Though he seemed nice enough, the green-haired weirdo wore a tuxedo jacket over his coveralls.

Here's an example from another critique submission:

> Luke **believed** that his dad knew most everything that went on in Willacy County but he **wasn't sure** he knew about the sugarcane fields.

Now, without the thinker attributives:

> Luke's dad knew most everything that went on in Willacy County, except maybe about the sugarcane fields.

Because the passage is written from Luke's viewpoint, these are clearly Luke's thoughts, though he might be wrong about what his father knows or doesn't know.

As with thinker attributives, minimize the use of italics. Use it only for direct thoughts, as in this example from a critique submission:

Is there another exit? I can't remember.

Italic text is difficult to read. If you italicize every thought your character has, you'll try your reader's patience. Whenever possible, convert direct thoughts to indirect thoughts and express them in plain text:

I couldn't remember if there was another exit.

Here's another example from the same submission:

I guess purists would say this cathedral is too much of a mélange of styles. I disagree. I like it because it reflects the varied history of its builders.

Now, as an indirect thought:

Purists would say this cathedral was too much of a mélange of styles, but to me it reflected the varied history of its builders.

Comparisons

When you use comparisons (metaphors or similes), you draw for your reader a mental picture that relates your story element to something within the reader's realm of experience.

Consider the following passage, in which several characters cross an open expanse of the Moon's surface toward a building:

> ... the four of them made a dash for the building. They ran side by side. In the Moon's gravity, they rose slowly with each stride, and returned to the ground just as slowly, only to bounce again and again until they reached their destination.

This passage contains a detailed description of how my characters run in the low gravity. It tries to evoke an image that will bring the setting to life and show how the Moon is unlike Earth. The problem is, I've used so many words that by the time the reader reaches the end of the description, he no longer cares about the image. He just wants to get on with the story. Comparing the characters' motion to something familiar can evoke the desired image much more clearly, and with fewer words, than literal description:

> ... the four of them made a dash for the building, bounding up and down in a ragged line **like so many horses on a merry-go-round.**

Taking a merry-go-round out of context, putting it on the Moon, and using it to describe running makes the comparison unexpected. I've used a familiar object to show how my setting is different from the reader's here-and-now.

Yet I can improve the passage further. The word *building* by itself isn't very descriptive. How big is this building? What does it look like? I've missed an opportunity to remind the reader that I've taken him to another world. In an earlier scene, I described the building like this:

> The habitation dome was maybe a hundred meters in diameter with the semicylindrical protrusion of the equipment garage on one side, the only obvious entrance to the structure.

Can you picture the building? What if I add this sentence:

> From afar, it looked **like a giant igloo on a vast stretch
> of dirty ice.**

The comparison solidifies the image. In *Worlds Asunder,* I refer
back to this description in the merry-go-round scene by changing
the word *building* to *igloo:*

> … the four of them made a dash for the igloo, bounding up
> and down in a ragged line like so many horses on a merry-
> go-round.

You can use comparisons to evoke emotion. Consider this description of the *Phoenix* crash site:

> As Chase drew closer, the fuselage came into view, jut-
> ting skyward from the flat terrain, surrounded by sparkling
> debris.

Perhaps this evokes an image, but I can enhance the emotional
impact with a couple of well-drawn comparisons:

> As Chase drew closer, the fuselage came into view, jutting
> skyward from the flat terrain **like a solitary tombstone in
> a field of glittering metal.**

When the fuselage becomes a tombstone in a field, it forms the
emotional image of a grave. It reminds the reader of something
he already knows: A body lies here, probably inside the fuselage.

Comparisons can be used to express an idea or a character's
mindset more effectively than direct narrative can, as shown in
this example from *Worlds Asunder.*

> Minutes later, a tremendous pop reverberated through
> the cavernous hangar from the huge doors in front of the

cockpit window. The squeal of the unused rollers filtered into the cabin **like a scream of protest** against this change in military posture.

This passage doesn't specify what the change in military posture is. Nevertheless, when I use "scream of protest" to describe a simple sound, I don't have to tell the reader how the viewpoint character feels about the change.

Look for opportunities to use comparison, but don't overdo it. A well-placed comparison that evokes the right image, at the right time, will enrich your story. But if every paragraph contains one, you'll force too many unrelated images upon the reader. Your own story will get lost among them.

Beware of misused, imprecise, or clichéd comparisons. Misused or imprecise comparisons can confuse your reader. Clichéd comparisons will have no emotional impact.

Specificity

Populate your world with specific, concrete details. Doing so is the surest way to capture your reader's imagination. It makes your world real.

Consider the following passage from *Venus Rain*:

Amanda moved away from the dangerous **equipment** to a safer location near the wall.

Does the word *equipment* evoke an image or emotion? Does it reveal anything about Amanda or the world in which she lives? Does it bring the story to life? No, because it's not specific.

Real life isn't populated with vague references. We use them in our speech when we think the listener knows what we're referring to, but your reader is not like a listener. Your reader doesn't know your world. You must show it to her.

Watch what happens when I replace the equipment and dangers in this scene with specific details:

> **Liquid helium** whistled past the **breached valve** with the wail of a wounded banshee, **272 degrees below zero,** cold enough to freeze human flesh in microseconds. Amanda dove for the far wall, where the stream of evaporating helium dissipated into the heat of the **temperature-moderated maintenance chamber.** Just beyond the bulkhead, **super-heated gasses,** the lifeblood of the terraforming project, roared through **pipes as big around as a docking collar.** An **incessant, numbing vibration** shook the floor.

This example demonstrates how a few well-placed specifics can transform a passage from a mere silhouette of reality into a crafted narrative that reveals character and setting in a way that evokes images and emotions from the reader.

The following example, also from *Venus Rain,* illustrates the value of specificity in details unrelated to setting:

> The money was good, or good enough at any rate. With overtime, it paid **the bills,** so Amanda worked her ass off and kept her mouth shut.

This passages shows how Amanda feels about her job, and it shows that she's a workaholic. Yet, look what I can accomplish by replacing the word *bills* with something more specific:

> The money was good, or good enough at any rate. It paid **her son's medical bills and her daughter's tuition,** if she put in enough hours. So she worked her ass off, kept her mouth shut, and prayed that she'd have enough at the end of the month for **the rent, the sustenance charge, and the Project tax.**

This not only shows something about Amanda, but about her kids as well. And it shows how the world I've created differs from the one in which the reader lives. Sustenance charge? Project tax? We don't have those today. At least not yet.

Here's an example from *Worlds Asunder*. An early draft read:

President Powers was **working** at her desk.

Apply specificity and this simple image becomes interesting:

President Powers glanced up from **the latest version of the Transatlantic Mass Transit Proposal.**

Find the vague words in your writing and make them specific.

Verb Choice

When a reader buys your book, he's buying your passion, your emotion. Your verbs not only carry the action, they carry the passion.

Examine each and every verb in your manuscript, including those you've upgraded from to-be verbs to active verbs. Make each the *right verb* for the sentence, the verb that most conveys the mood of the scene and the emotions of the viewpoint character.

Consider these lines:

Clark **hung onto** the side of the cliff.

Clark **clung** to the side of the cliff.

The verb *clung* communicates a greater degree of urgency and desperation than *hung onto* does. If that's what your scene warrants, use it.

Select verbs that evoke an image. I wrote the following sentence in an early draft of *Venus Rain*:

Professor La Roche **made his way** down the stairs to the front row of seats.

Walked would have been better than *made his way*. At least then the reader would know La Roche is on his feet. Yet there are so many ways to walk: stroll, saunter, march, pace, tiptoe, etc. Each brings to mind a different image of La Roche "making his way" down the stairs.

In the book, a brutal tyrant has just put a bullet through the head of one of La Roche's colleagues during a speech La Roche was giving. Based on the advice of a critiquer, I revised the verb in my original sentence:

> Professor La Roche **staggered** down the stairs to the front row of seats.

Staggered provokes a stronger emotional response from the reader than *made his way* or even *walked* does, especially given the context.

Give each verb in your manuscript this kind of careful consideration.

Not and *n't*

Readers want to know what something is. On a subconscious level, they'll be dissatisfied if you tell them only what something is not.[1] Therefore, *not interesting*, becomes *uninteresting, boring, dull,* or *plain*; perhaps even *uninspired, bland,* or *tedious*, depending on the context.

I revised the following example passages in *Worlds Asunder*:

This:	**Became:**
• ... not much more than a couple of habitation tents.	• ... just a couple of habitation tents.
• ... taking care not to disturb the bits of evidence he passed along the way.	• ... taking care to avoid the bits of evidence he passed along the way.
• ... he ordered them to stay sober and not leave the base.	• ... he ordered them to stay sober and confined them to the base.
• ... not within its line of sight.	• ... out of its line of sight.

Generally speaking, eliminating *not* results in tighter, more precise wording.

Minimize your usage of the word *not*. Search your manuscript electronically for the word *not*, including the contraction *n't*. Use the Find/Replace function of your word processor to change the text format of these words to a different color (say, green). Doing so will help you find them during editing. Once you've finished revising, Select All and change the text back to black.

That

The word *that* is often used unnecessarily. It becomes a speed bump that slows the reader down.

Consider the following example, excerpted from a letter Chase wrote to his daughter in *Worlds Asunder*:

> I'm writing to let you know **that** my homecoming will be delayed. I know **that** you and the girls were looking forward to seeing me, but a case has come up **that** will delay my departure.

Wherever you see the word *that* in your manuscript, delete it and read the sentence *out loud* without it. If the sentence makes sense, leave out the word *that*. In this example, only the third *that* is necessary.

> I'm writing to let you know my homecoming will be delayed. I know you and the girls were looking forward to seeing me, but a case has come up **that** will delay my departure.

Search your manuscript electronically for the word *that*. Use the Find/Replace function of your word processor to change the text format of these words to a different color (say, pink). Doing so will help you find them during editing. Once you've finished revising, Select All and change the text back to black.

Clichés

Clichéd phrases signal a clichéd mindset to editors and agents,[2] who will assume this mindset permeates every element of your writing, such as character and plot. Furthermore, a novel rife with clichés will fail to provoke original images in the mind of your reader.

The first draft of *Venus Rain* contained this phrase:

> ... stuck out like a sore thumb.

Of course, I recognized the phrase as a cliché as soon as I wrote it, but I was caught in the throes of writing my first draft and didn't stop to conceive something better. Later, however, I revised the passage:

> ... stood out like a Jovian moon in the Terran sky.

This is both fresher and more appropriate to the science fiction genre and to the character's viewpoint.

Beware clichéd phrases like the ones listed in Figure 6.[3] Search for these electronically and purge them from your manuscript.

This is not by any means an all-inclusive list, nor is it intended to be. I provide it for the sole purpose of getting you into the mindset of looking for clichés. It seems to work. As I write this paragraph after composing the list, I wonder if "by any means," "all-inclusive list," "for the sole purpose," and "getting into the mindset" ought to be included.

Repeated Elements

Repeated elements are aspects of your story, particularly an emotion or bit of characterization, that you've shown in more than one way. Similar to repeated information, repeated elements weaken your writing.

Clichés

Add insult to injury

All else being equal

All things considered

Along those lines

Ample opportunity

Armed to the teeth

As a matter of fact

At a loss for words

At long last

Benefit of the doubt

Better late than never

Bone of contention

Break the bank

By the same token

Calling names

Chop up the small fry

Crying need

Cut a deal

Drastic action

Every trough has a bottom

Exercise in futility

Existing conditions

Eyes like twin lasers

Festive occasion

Filled to capacity

Food for thought

Foregone conclusion

Foreseeable future

Get our feet back under us

Give him/her/me a hand

Give the green light

Grave concern

Green with envy

Hate his/her/their guts

Hate with a passion

Heart's desire

Heated argument

In no uncertain terms

In short supply

In this day and age

It goes without saying

It's not rocket science

Just desserts

Leave no stone unturned

Leave well enough alone

Lend a helping hand

Living on borrowed time

Love so much it hurts

Mad as a hatter

Mad as hell

Moment of truth

More than meets the eye

Narrow escape

Needs no introduction

Of paramount importance

Only a matter of time

One and the same

Overwhelming odds

Own worst enemy

Paper over the cracks

Part and parcel

Path of least resistance

Pointing fingers

Remedy the situation

Ride the tiger

Ripe old age

Rob Peter to pay Paul

Round of applause

Second to none

Select few

Shocked silence

Shot in the arm

Sleeping giant

Stick out like a sore thumb

Sweeping changes

The joker in the deck

The ticking clock

The wheels came off

Too numerous to mention

Two-edged sword

Two-sided coin

Until the bitter end

Untimely end

Viable alternative

Walk on water

Wave of the future

Whole new ball game

With all due respect

With all my heart

With due consideration

Figure 6. Clichés[3]

The following examples are from a critique submission:

> Cynmar **noted** and **analyzed** …

> … **pulled, turned** and **twisted, bucked** and **bumped,**
> along a very specific path …

> … would **fight dirty** and **play foul** …

> … they seemed to be in **fear, awe, wonder**, and a touched
> **bewildered** by …

If you've repeated an element, determine which passage shows
it in the most effective way, then delete the rest.

Unintentionally repeated elements aren't always obvious.
They can be difficult for even experienced writers to catch for
themselves.

Can you spot the repeated element in the following passage
from an early draft of *Worlds Asunder*?

> When he rounded to the back of the ship, he came up short.
> The sparsely scattered debris field spanned a kilometer or
> more in each direction. Footprints lay everywhere among
> the wreckage, wandering from scrap to scrap as though
> seeking some special trinket.

If you said, "Footprints lay everywhere among the wreckage"
and "wandering from scrap to scrap," you're right. Though these
are not equivalent statements, they serve the same purpose in
the narrative. As such, they weaken one another. The question is:
Which one should I keep? I deleted the latter, mainly because it's
inaccurate. Footprints don't wander. People do.

> Footprints lay everywhere among the wreckage as
> though the person who'd left them had sought some
> special souvenir.

Here's another one. See if you can spot the repeated element:

> There was a loud shuffling as the twenty or so crewmen rose and filed out of the briefing room to congregate in the hall. The men and three women of the covert space plane project gathered to speculate among themselves about what it all meant. Bill looked for Ted Branson, the mission specialist of one of the teams that hadn't been assigned to the mission, and a close friend. "Ted, let me see your thinpad for a second."

The repeated elements are "congregate in the hall" and "gathered to speculate." One says where, the other says why, but both show people standing together. Because the dialogue that follows this paragraph shows the reason for their congregation, I removed the second phrase and left the first:

> There was a loud shuffling as twenty-one crewmen rose and filed out of the briefing room to congregate in the hall. Bill looked for Ted Branson, the mission specialist of one of the standby teams. "Ted, let me see your thinpad a second."

This example from a fight scene in *Worlds Asunder* contains two repeated elements, one in each paragraph:

> **The whole apartment seemed to be swirling.** Nothing was clear and **everything was moving**. *Where is he?*
> Chase heard a sound to his left and spun his head. For a moment, **his vision went black**, the swift movement **nearly causing him to lose consciousness.**

This revision eliminates the repeats:

> The whole apartment seemed to be swirling.
> Chase heard a sound to the left and spun his head.

For a moment, his vision went black and the pain in his
skull soared.

Repeated elements can involve whole scenes. In *Worlds Asunder,*
I included two scenes in which Snider forced Chase into a press
briefing Chase wasn't prepared to give. The first was merely a few
quick comments when Chase returned from the crash site. The
second became the chapter-long press conference in which I revealed Chase's history with the *Phoenix* pilot.

A critiquer rightfully cited these scenes as repetitive, though one
encompassed only a few paragraphs. To remedy this, I had Chase
refuse Snider's initial request to talk to the press. This avoids repetition. Furthermore, having Chase refuse Snider's demand shows
a strength of character lacking in the original version.

Often, repeated elements take the form of showing something
and then telling it, as in the following passage from a critique
submission:

Jackal let out a derisive snort. "Don't you play dumb with
me, vamp. **You killed one of my pack last night.**"
**So it did have something to do with the guy Jason
had killed.**

The second paragraph tells what the first shows. This problem
is easy to correct. Keep the words that show and delete the ones
that tell:

Jackal let out a derisive snort. "Don't you play dumb with
me, vamp. You killed one of my pack last night."

At best, repeated elements give the feel of wordiness to your
narrative. At worst, they condescend to the reader. Have confidence in your ability to show. Show things once and show them
well. The reader will get the point.

Repeated Words

The following passage from an early draft of *Worlds Asunder* takes place immediately after a lunar building explodes. A construction worker drives his oversized bulldozer up a damaged truck ramp and spots two wounded survivors trapped on a damaged framework of trusses above him:

> **He** depressurized his compartment and climbed out. When he saw the distance he had to jump, he found it to be greater than he'd expected. **He** heard the men above him now, coming in loud and clear on his comm system, urging him to hurry. **He** looked up and saw their catwalk swaying and beginning to sag under their weight.
>
> **He** took a deep breath, bent his legs and jumped. **He** cleared the distance with little trouble, but the structure sagged beneath him as he landed. **He** lost his balance, coming down hard on the metal grid that constituted the catwalk floor. **He** slid backwards toward the six-story drop that he had just leapt. There were no handholds to grasp. The gloves of the EVA were too bulky and cumbersome to find purchase. **He** slid from the walkway until he was off the edge before his hand grasped the loose railing. His weight caused that too, to bend, but he managed to retain his grip.

Eight of the twelve sentences in this passage start with *he*. This draws the reader's attention away from the story and onto the text. Furthermore, repeated sentence beginnings may signal an action scene that focuses on the events rather than on the character.

Restructure your sentences to avoid repeated beginnings. Include more sensory details. Show your viewpoint character's emotions. The following revision doesn't have a single sentence that begins with *he*:

Once in place, he depressurized the compartment and climbed out. His heart sank when he saw the distance he'd have to jump.

The men called to him through the comm, urging him to hurry. Suddenly, a support buckled and the whole catwalk began to give under their weight.

Horace took a deep breath and leapt the four-story drop, sailing gracelessly across the gap to the trusswork with centimeters to spare. The structure sagged beneath him and he crashed to the grid-metal floor of the walk. With few handholds and gloves too bulky to find purchase, he slid off the edge. At the last instant, his hand found a loose railing, and his weight caused that, too, to bend. But he managed to retain his grip.

Similarly, don't repeat the same uncommon word within a short span of text. Consider the following examples excerpted from a critique submission:

"James, could you close the door **a bit**. I love a summer breeze but it is **a bit** chilly tonight ..."

Jamie, Leah, Camille, and Lawrence **passed** the platter around, fast and deliberate, like a quarterback **passing** off a football.

Like repeated sentence beginnings, repeated words draw the reader's attention to the text. Substitute synonyms to avoid repeating words or, as in the second passage, to avoid using a different form of the same root word:

"James, could you close the door. I love a summer breeze but it's **a bit** chilly tonight ..."

Jamie, Leah, Camille, and Lawrence **passed** the platter around, fast and deliberate, like a quarterback **handing-off** a football.

Adverbs   *NO "LY" words*

In general, delete your adverbs. These often end in *ly* and usually modify a verb, though they can also modify an adjective or another adverb. Adverbs tend to signify lazy writing. The author uses a descriptor to avoid finding the right verb. I once heard a writer recommend deleting *all* adverbs from a manuscript and reading it without them, then putting back only those that are absolutely necessary. I would add: For those that remain, strengthen the verb rather than reinsert the adverb.

This:	**Might become:**
• Stared **grumpily**	• Glared, glowered, scowled, or frowned
• Accused **lightly**	• Teased, implicated, or reproached

Consider this example from a critique submission:

> Matt's scraggly brown hair bounced **slightly** while he talked **animatedly** …

This might become:

> Matt's scraggly brown hair bounced while he prattled …

Sometimes, as in "bounced slightly," the verb choice is appropriate and the adverb is superfluous. In this case, leave the verb alone and delete the adverb.

Search your manuscript electronically for *ly*. Use the Find/Replace function of your word processor to change the text format of these letters to a different color (say, red). Doing so will help you find them during editing. Do this for the words *too, very,* and *just* as well. Once you've finished revising, Select All and change the text back to black.

If you choose to use a thesaurus, *The Synonym Finder* by J. I. Rodale and Nancy LaRoche is the best I've found. Beware the thesaurus, however. Don't use it just to find a fancy alternative. Choose a word because it means exactly what you want to convey to the reader.

Adjectives

Adjectives are often used to prop up weak nouns that should be strengthened to stand on their own. Furthermore, don't string a bunch of adjectives together to describe a single noun:

> ... a **hot**, **dry**, **sunny**, **summer** day.

The use of multiple adjectives gives the reader too much information to catalogue, especially if you do it often. If you must use an adjective, limit yourself to one per noun. Pick the one that describes the characteristic most important to the viewpoint character. For example, a construction worker laboring outside would probably describe the day as hot. A farmer, concerned about another year of drought, would characterize the day as dry.

Read through your manuscript for unnecessary adjectives or adjectives that are too common, and eliminate them.

Prepositional Phrases

> Chase stood **among the clues in the cockpit** and let them tell their story.

If the reader already knows Chase is in the cockpit, write this as:

> Chase stood **among the clues** and let them tell their story.

Depending on the context, the following might be sufficient:

> Chase let the clues tell their story.

Unnecessary prepositional phrases come across as repetitive and wordy. Challenge each prepositional phrase in your manuscript. If it doesn't say something that's both new and necessary, delete it.

Anachronism

In Chapter 9, I discussed anachronism within the content of your scenes. Now look for it in your word choice. Some words and phrases develop over time, others evolve from technology. "Derailed," for example, emerged from the railroad industry. Don't use it — or others like "blowing off steam," "train of thought," or "one-track mind" — in any context if your story takes place before the invention of the railroad.

If you're writing a historical piece, buy a dictionary that includes the date of origin of each word. Look up any questionable words. Make sure they didn't originate later.

Today, the word *scan* often means "to convert a document from hardcopy to electronic form using a scanner," but according to the Merriam-Webster on-line dictionary, it has many meanings, including "to read hastily." The word has been around since the fourteenth century. So in a Renaissance novel, a character may *scan* a document, but in an earlier historical piece, he might *look over* the document instead.

Avoid slang terms. Slang is particularly prone to anachronism because it changes rapidly. It can date your novel. Furthermore, slang words change meaning quickly over time, so they may confuse your next-generation readers.

Wordiness

Eliminate unnecessary words.

Consider these examples from a critique submission:

This:	**Might become:**
• … as if whatever had been causing the noise had detected his gaze.	• … as if whatever caused it detected his gaze.
• … made him feel a bit breathless …	• … snatched his breath …
• The person that was standing in front of him . . .	• The intruder …

Concise writing will create a greater emotional impact than verbose prose. It's more clear, easier to read, and will increase the pace of the story.

Pronoun Antecedents

Every pronoun must refer to a preceding noun, called its antecedent. Grammatically, the antecedent is the noun most recently mentioned in the text that matches the pronoun in gender (if applicable) and number (singular or plural).

Read the following passage from an early draft of *Worlds Asunder*:

> [Chase] handed [Michelle] a crate.
> She eyed both him and the box with apprehension. "What is it?"
> "Samples. I'd like you to take them to the materials lab and work with the **techs**. **They**'re all labeled."

In the last sentence, what are labeled? The samples or the techs? I meant the samples, but grammatically, the antecedent of "they" is "the techs." I rearranged the passage to place the pronoun closer to its antecedent:

"**Samples. They**'re all labeled. Take them to the materials lab and work with the techs ..."

Failure to attend to pronoun antecedents can produce laughable results. An early draft of *Venus Rain* contained the sentence:

La Roche took off his glasses, wiped his **eyes** on his sleeve and replaced **them**.

David J. Corwell, one of my critiquers, rightfully commented:

"Them" refers back to "eyes," which gave me the crazy image of La Roche popping out his eyes and sticking new ones in.

Obviously, this isn't the image I had in mind. It's not the one I got when I read the passage, because I knew what I was *trying* to say.

Often, the passage can be corrected by replacing the pronoun with the noun it refers to:

La Roche took of his glasses, wiped his eyes on his sleeve and replaced **his glasses**.

In this case, however, it seemed awkward to repeat *his glasses* in the same sentence, so I settled on the following revision:

La Roche took off his glasses and wiped his eyes with his sleeve.

He puts his glasses back on a few paragraphs later.

This example illustrates the importance of having a critiquer to catch the things you'll miss in your own writing. I'll discuss critiques in Chapter 15.

Questions in Your Character's Thoughts

Minimize the number of questions that appear in your character's thoughts. Similar to telling, questions in a character's thoughts do your reader's work for her. They tell her what to wonder. Let the reader come up with her own questions.

Consider the following passage from a critique submission, in which Luke has ventured into a sugarcane field that has always frightened him. There, he meets a boy named Antonio.

> The dark-haired Mexican kid was standing with a finger over his lips.
>
> Luke frowned and opened his mouth.
>
> The boy shook his head and made a waving motion.
>
> **He wants me to go away?** That's what I'm trying to do. **Why did he stop me?** Luke studied Antonio. He's trying to hide something. **But what? Himself?** This kid is confused, Luke thought. Antonio must be an illegal. **What else could he be hiding?**

The last paragraph puts direct questions into Luke's thoughts. There's almost always a more effective way to show what questions your character faces than to pose them so blatantly:

> The dark-haired Mexican kid stood with a finger over his lips.
>
> Luke frowned and opened his mouth.
>
> The boy shook his head and made a waving motion to shoo Luke away.
>
> All Luke wanted to do was run, to get as far from this creepy cane field as possible by the time the dying sun faded from the horizon. Yet he studied Antonio. Nobody would enter the sugarcane, especially at night, unless he was hiding something. He must be an illegal.

The reader still knows what questions Luke has. Now, however, the reasons for them are clear as well.

Subtlety

Subtlety is the mark of an experienced writer. It signals confidence, not only in oneself as a writer, but also in the reader as a perceptive, intelligent individual.[4] If you spell everything out, you'll risk boring her. Readers want to be intrigued. They want to think. In an extreme case, a lack of subtlety may insult your reader, like when you tell something that you've already shown or use narration to explain a passage of dialogue.

Give your reader 2 + 2. Let her come up with 4 on her own. Show her an image, a thought, or an idea and let her imagination take it from there.

Consider this passage from *Worlds Asunder*:

> He'd have to start packing soon. Maybe tomorrow he'd crate up the nonessentials: his drawing table, most of his clothes, even that ridiculous hologram Erin sent him last year, the one that misrepresented Pluto's orbit. Eventually everything would go, except for the framed DeMitri on the far wall. Painted to make use of the base's high-ceilinged lunar architecture, it was too big to take back to Earth. Besides, he'd have little need for an Earthly landscape of the Olympic Range when he could look upon it with his own eyes.

In this passage, I carefully selected belongings that would imply meaning beyond that which I've actually stated.

The painting, for example, does a couple of things. It suggests where Chase is moving to: Seattle, near the Olympic mountain range. It also shows how architecture on the Moon differs from architecture on Earth: high ceilings to accommodate the leaping strides necessary in low gravity. Notice, however, that the passage doesn't say why the ceilings are high. I let the reader figure that out on her own.

Chase doesn't like the hologram, yet he plans to keep it. This shows that Erin, whom the reader will later learn is Chase's daughter, is important to him.

Furthermore, Chase recognizes that the hologram displays Pluto's orbit incorrectly. Pluto does have an odd orbit; therefore, it's a credible mistake. Here, I show that Chase knows with confidence that the hologram is wrong. The reader will later learn that he was the first man to orbit Pluto.

Will the reader pick up on these subtle implications? Who knows? They're there for those who care to contemplate them.

Clarity

When you write, be clear. This doesn't contradict the previous section. Subtlety is a good thing. Give your reader something to pick up on the second time she reads your book; that's always nice. Don't write a passage that simply doesn't make sense. Consider this passage from a fairly polished, post-critique version of *Worlds Asunder*. Several characters are discussing three terrorist-style attacks: the sabotage of the *Phoenix*, a fire in a hangar bay at Lunar Alpha Base, and a bombing at a lunar mine nearly halfway around the Moon.

Chase shrugged. "Sounds like we don't know much about the fire. What about Montanari?"

"All we know is what we saw on the newsblips," Brower said. "A mine employee, a Chinese national named Zhou Zheming, climbed into a fuel tanker with a case of mining explosives, drove it into the new helium plant, and blew it up." He still spoke in a belligerent tone. "Structural damage was significant but repairable. Reports indicate anywhere from three to eight people injured. Zhou Zheming was the only fatality."

"Maybe it wasn't the same person." Michelle spoke quietly.

"That's possible," Chase agreed. "In fact, if there haven't been any shuttles from here to the mine since the fire, then it must be someone else."

Though this passage seemed clear to me, it wasn't clear to my editor, Susan Grossman. Look at it again, this time with Susan's comments (inserted in bold text):

"Maybe it wasn't the same person." Michelle spoke quietly. **[Maybe who wasn't the same person?]**
"That's possible," Chase agreed. "In fact, if there haven't been any shuttles from here to the mine since the fire, then it must be someone else." **[I don't understand what this statement is getting at.]**

A few paragraphs later, Susan wrote:

I'm finding this chapter confusing.

Based on her comments, I revised the dialogue to bolster the clarity of the exchange:

Michelle spoke quietly, almost to herself. "Even if the three crimes are connected, they may not have been committed by the same person."
"That's possible," Chase agreed. "In fact, if there haven't been any shuttles from here to the mine since the fire, the bombing must have been committed by a second person."

In all passages, make your writing clear.

Verb Tense
Use consistent verb tense. In this example from a critique submission, the author mixes past and present tense. The result is an awkward, grammatically incorrect narrative.

> He **wore** [past tense] a leather pack to which an assort-
> ment of items **were** [past tense] tightly tied ... Turning back
> to the trail, he **descends** [present tense] ...

This writer could have used present tense:

> He **wears** a leather pack to which an assortment of items
> **are** tightly tied ... Turning back to the trail, he **descends** ...

Most fiction writers, however, use past tense:

> He **wore** a leather pack to which an assortment of
> items **were** tightly tied ... Turning back to the trail, he
> **descended** ...

Either way, choose a verb tense and stick with it.

Paragraph Breaks

Consider the following passage from *Worlds Asunder*, in which Chase
assesses the aftermath of a brief gunfight in the enemy stronghold:

> Hundreds of dents puckered the enviro-dome from enemy
> bullets, but the structure took the damage without breach.
> The militants must have anticipated the possibility of dis-
> covery and assault when they built the complex. None of
> Chase's team had been hit. Three of the bodies lay at the
> other end of the hall, but one sprawled in front of Chase.
> There was no way to know if he had killed the man or if
> Gloria had. He tried to tell himself that it didn't matter; in
> combat, one did what one must to survive.

The length of this paragraph slows the pace of the narrative.
The paragraph should therefore be divided into smaller chunks.
To do this, look for logical breaks based on content. Here, the
first part of the paragraph discusses structural damage to the
building; the rest describes the human casualties:

Hundreds of dents puckered the enviro-dome from enemy bullets, but the structure took the damage without breach. The militants must have anticipated the possibility of discovery and assault when they built the complex.

None of Chase's team had been hit.

Three of the bodies lay at the other end of the hall, but one sprawled in front of Chase. There was no way to know if he had killed the man or if Gloria had. He tried to tell himself that it didn't matter; in combat, one did what one must to survive.

I gave the comment about Chase's team a paragraph of its own. This emphasizes the importance of the statement.

Although the text of the second passage is identical to that of the first, the more frequent paragraph breaks increase the apparent pace of the narrative.

Make sure your paragraph breaks are appropriate, based on content, desired emphasis, and pacing.

Punctuation

The punctuation errors discussed below are the ones I most commonly see in critique submissions from amateur writers. Check your manuscript for these and other punctuation problems.

1   Semicolon (;)

In fiction, the semicolon is used for one of two purposes. First, it can connect two closely linked sentences. Use it sparingly. Your reader will assume two consecutive sentences are related unless you separate them by a paragraph break, so a semicolon is rarely needed. Use it only when a period may cause confusion about your meaning.

Use the semicolon only to link two independent clauses. If the clause on either side of the semicolon is dependent, insert a comma instead of a semicolon.

Second, use the semicolon to delineate a list that

contains one or more sub-lists, as in the following passage from *Worlds Asunder.*

> "Also on the list are David Herrera; Jack Snider; Stan Brower; Randy Lauback and Phyllis Conway, the **Phoenix** crew; Julie Chavez and Avery Robinson, the traffic controllers on duty; and anybody who had access to the online passenger list." He looked up. "I was surprised to find that it reflected the change."

If I had used a comma in place of each semicolon, the passage would have indicated that Randy Lauback and Phyllis Conway were on the list *in addition to* the *Phoenix* crew. With the semicolon, it becomes clear that Randy and Phyllis are on the list *as* the *Phoenix* crew. The same is true for the traffic controllers, Julie Chavez and Avery Robinson.

2 Parentheses ( )

Avoid parentheses in fiction writing. Use commas to offset parenthetical phrases.

3 Em-dash (—)

Use the em-dash to insert an explanation into the middle of a sentence, or to append an afterthought:

> I don't know much about the case yet — I'm leaving for the accident site even as I write this letter — but if it's as bad as I believe, you'll see it in the newsblips.

Use the em-dash only when the explanation or afterthought is an independent clause. Compare the following examples. In the first, the appended clause is independent. In the second, it's dependent, so I've used a comma instead.

A freighter, the record said. Local — its operations were restricted to lunar destinations.

A freighter, the record said. Local, its operations restricted to lunar destinations.

The em-dash has another important use in dialogue, which I'll discuss in Chapter 12.

Exclamation Point (!)

Don't use exclamation points in narration. Use them sparingly, if at all, in your character's thoughts. In dialogue, the exclamation point denotes shouting. Thoughts are silent.

If you struggle with punctuation, buy a good book on the subject and refer to it often. I use *Merriam-Webster's Pocket Guide to Punctuation*.

Exercises

1   Select a scene you've written. Search it electronically for to-be verbs. Change their font color to blue. Search for the word *not* (including the contraction *n't*). Change the color of these words to green. Search for adverbs (for *ly, too, just,* and *very*). Change these characters and words to red text.

Which colors are prominent on the page? These represent potential weaknesses in your writing style. Revise the scene to purge 75% of your to-be verbs and 90% of the words in red or green text. Have someone read both versions of the scene. Ask the reader which she liked better and why.

2   Select a scene you've written. Highlight any sentence that uses the word *as* or an *-ing* verb to put a bit of action into a subordinate clause. In another color, highlight every prepositional phrase. Highlight adjectives in a third color and every instance of the word *that* in a fourth.

Examine your as-ing sentences. Have you implied that sequential actions are occurring simultaneously or provided both a beat and an attributive for the same line of dialogue? If so, restructure the sentence to correct it. Now reduce the remaining as-ing sentences to only two per manuscript-formatted page. (Formatting is discussed in Chapter 14.)

Challenge each prepositional phrase. Does it provide information that is both new and necessary? If not, delete it. Delete any adjective beyond one per noun. Delete every unnecessary *that*. Have someone read both versions of the scene. Ask the reader which he liked better and why.

3   Select a scene you've written. In four different colors, highlight thinker attributes, filter words, questions that appear in your character's thoughts, and clichéd phrases.

Which colors are prominent on the page? These represent weaknesses in your writing style. Rewrite the scene to eliminate *all* of the highlighted words and phrases. Have someone read both versions. Ask the reader which she liked better and why.

4   Select a scene you've written. In three different colors, highlight all verbs, nouns, and pronouns. For each verb, challenge yourself to come up with a stronger, more precise verb. Is the verb tense correct? If not, correct it. For each noun, challenge yourself to find a more specific noun. For each pronoun, make sure its antecedent is correct. If it's not, correct it. Rewrite the scene using your new word choices. Have someone read both versions of the scene. Ask the reader which he liked better and why.

5   Select a scene you've written. Rewrite each sentence using as few words as possible. Look for opportunities to use comparisons to reduce the need for description. Delete any repeated elements. Try to reduce your total word count by 25% without sacrificing meaning. Make sure the meaning of each sentence is clear. Have someone read both versions of the scene. Ask the reader which she liked better and why.

6   Select a scene you've written. Make all the changes described in Exercises 1 through 5 to the same scene. Have someone read both versions. Ask the reader which he liked better and why.

7   Select five clichés from the list in Figure 6. For each one, write a short passage (no more than a paragraph or two in length) that uses the cliché in some sort of context. Now replace each cliché with something more original.

12

Dialogue

Realistic dialogue is one of the most difficult things for some writers to achieve. It's also one of the most important. Many editors and agents, when they receive a submission, will read a section of dialogue first. If it's good, they'll consider the manuscript. If not, they'll reject it without a second thought.[1]

So what is realistic dialogue?

When people talk, they ramble, they pause, they repeat themselves — they say all sorts of unnecessary things. Written dialogue that includes all this stuff will be cumbersome. Your reader won't have the patience for it. The objective of dialogue is to make it more efficient than normal speech yet still have it sound realistic. This is what makes dialogue a challenge.

As I recommended with your scenes and prose, edit your dialogue for only one thing at a time, but don't go on to the next passage until you've edited the current passage for each potential problem listed in the following sections.

Everyday Dialogue

Everyday dialogue refers to the pleasantries every reader knows occur at the beginning and end of a conversation:

"Hi."
"How are you?"
"I'm fine. How are you?"

Get rid of it. It's boring. Start the conversation at the point where it becomes interesting. Here's an example of everyday dialogue from an early draft of *Worlds Asunder*:

> The comm panel buzzed.
>
> Chase reached over and pressed the speaker button. "**Yeah**?"
>
> "**Morgan**?" the caller asked.
>
> "**Yeah**." Chase repeated.
>
> "**Morgan, this is Stan Brower.** The *Phoenix* is in trouble. She's lost her thrust control. It looks like she's going down. Snider has asked for you to assemble a team and head out to the site for the investigation."

Revised, this scene reads:

> The comm panel buzzed. Chase stretched his lanky frame and got to his feet, then leapt to the terminal against the slight lunar g.
>
> He keyed the link. On the screen, a frown elongated the narrow face of Security Chief Stan Brower, whose sharp eyes were nearly as pale as his graying hair. This wouldn't be good news.
>
> "We've got a ship in trouble," Brower said. "The *Phoenix*. Snider needs you to assemble a team."

I replaced the everyday dialogue with a bit of characterization that reveals something about both Brower (his expression and a brief description) and Chase (his assessment of what Brower's expression means). The dialogue begins with, "We've got a ship in trouble." That's where the conversation gets interesting.

I also compressed the dialogue in the last paragraph — tightened the wording to give it more punch. I'll discuss compression later in this chapter.

Informative Dialogue

Never have a character say something that everybody in the conversation already knows. I discussed this in terms of "puppet scenes" in Chapter 6. Now look for it on a smaller scale.

Consider this passage from an early draft of *Worlds Asunder* in which Snider speaks with the manager of Stellarfare, a commuter starline:

> "May I remind you," Snider said, "that **NASA is your regulatory authority. I can revoke your license to fly from Lunar Alpha.**"
>
> "Don't bully me. **NASA is funded by taxation of the businesses that operate from its bases. Stellarfare alone supplies a third of that funding for Lunar Alpha. I'm sure you have the authority to revoke my license.** But it will be the last thing you do as director. And when your replacement arrives, Stellarfare will return to Lunar Alpha."

Both characters already know NASA is Stellarfare's regulatory authority, and they know how much funding Stellarfare supplies. The only person who doesn't know this is the reader. That's who these characters are talking to, not to each other. Never let your characters talk directly to your reader.

Informative dialogue can often be corrected by moving the information from the dialogue to the thoughts of your viewpoint character:

> "I'll revoke your license to fly from Lunar Alpha." Snider's voice shook with forced civility.
>
> "Don't bully me. Revoke our license and it'll be the last thing you do as director. When you're replaced, we'll return."
>
> He was right. Damn it, the manager was right. Stellarfare provided a third of NASA's funding for Lunar Alpha. Snider's threat had only solidified the man's resolve.

This revision allowed me to inject stronger emotion by adding:

> Snider's voice shook with forced civility.

This statement wouldn't have worked with dialogue that begins with the unemotional phrase:

> "May I remind you ... "

I'll discuss matching a character's dialogue and emotions later in this chapter.

Incidentally, phrases like "May I remind you ..." and "I'm sure you know ..." are red flags for informative dialogue.

Direct Address

Direct address occurs when a character says the name of the person he's addressing:

> "What time is it, **Jennifer**?"
> She consulted her watch. "Four o'clock, **Tommy**. Why?"
> "Already?" He snatched up his backpack and bolted for the door. "**Jennifer**, my mom's gonna kill me." He didn't even help clean up the toys they'd strewn across the living room.

Here, I've embedded the characters' names in the dialogue rather than putting them in tags. As a result, the dialogue rings false. Generally, people use direct address only when it's unclear which of several persons they're talking to.

Notice how much more natural the dialogue feels when I remove the characters' names from the spoken lines:

> "What time is it?" Tommy asked suddenly.
> Jennifer consulted her watch. "Four o'clock. Why?"
> "Already?" Tommy snatched up his backpack and bolted

for the door. "My mom's gonna kill me." He didn't even help clean up the toys they'd strewn across the living room.

Self-talk

Often, when a character talks to himself, the author is using contrived dialogue as a means to relay the character's thoughts to the reader, as is done in this passage from a critique submission:

> **"I feel like I've been run over by a Mac Truck,"** he moaned. **"Where am I anyway?"**
>
> He rolled his eyes from side to side and tried to think. **"I can't see a thing,"** he said aloud and tried to sit up again. This time the ground moved beneath him.
>
> **"Oh oh,"** he said. **"An earthquake?"** He tried to concentrate. **"Naw. It's not like that at all. It feels more like ball bearings rolling around under me."**
>
> The ground wiggled and shook under him once again.
>
> "Whoa." He caught his breath. **"This is not like anything I've ever felt before ..."**

Because your scene is written from your character's viewpoint, you can communicate his thoughts without having him say them out loud. Here's one way the author might eliminate the self-talk dialogue from the passage above:

> Luke's body ached like he'd been run over by a Mack Truck. He rolled his eyes from side to side in the darkness to clear his head.
>
> The earth began to shake. Not like an earthquake. More like ball bearings rolling around beneath him. "Whoa." It was the strangest thing he'd ever felt.

In addition, don't put your character's thoughts in quotation marks. Thoughts are thoughts, not dialogue.

Dialogue Compression

Cut any line of dialogue down to as few words as possible. Doing so will make it seem more natural and easier to read. Consider the following passage, excerpted (with spelling and grammar corrections) from a critique submission. The viewpoint character, Cynmar, observes this exchange between a young woman in a tavern and a druid who has just walked in.

One of the girls suddenly stood and waved at the shrouded figure. "Hey, Cuddles, it's Nancin! What are you doing here? Hey, this might just turn out to be some fun after all. We have to get together later on and catch up on old times. I haven't seen you since that party at Sister Hillary's Nunnery and Bawdy House back in '65. Come on up to my room when we get through with this rah-rah what-ever-it-is that's going on here and we'll crack a bottle or three and talk about old times - and more. Hot Damn, Cuddles is back, WHEEE!!!"

Cuddles? A low grade swinger who runs around with a magic staff of ash? This just does *not* add up. This whole mess is becoming more screwed up and twisted than a woodworkers brace and bits, Cynmar thought. Just who is this guy, and what is going on?

"Silence Woman! Hold your tongue. There is serious business afoot — and many unanswered questions. We will surely talk, later, and in private ..."

Her response was not quite what anyone expected, including by the one that was addressed. "Okay. I can wait for you to finish playing those 'serious business' games that you little boys insist on playing. Just don't forget that you and I have more important things to do." The soft purr of the reply held the promise of interesting times ahead.

This passage can and should be greatly compressed. In the first paragraph, Nancin rambles for far too long. The druid, a man of some renown, would probably be embarrassed by Nancin's outburst. He would likely stop her. I'd delete Cynmar's reaction entirely. The incongruity of the name "Cuddles" is obvious without it. The rest, I'd compress as much as possible *without sacrificing the essential voice of each character.*

> One of the girls stood and waved at the shrouded figure. "Hey, Cuddles. What are you doing here? This might just turn out to be some fun after all — "
> "Silence, woman," the druid said. "We'll talk later."
> "Okay," came the soft purr of her reply. "Just don't forget that you and I have more important things to do."

Decide for yourself which passage is more engaging.

Compression can make dialogue more crisp and realistic even in less extreme cases, as in these examples from *Worlds Asunder.*

This:	**Became:**
• "That's when the ship lost power so there was no electrical feedback to the unit beyond that time."	• "The ship lost power. There was no electrical feedback after that."
• "It should've picked up the cockpit conversation on backup battery power."	• "It should've picked up something on battery power."
• "Once you've got it in place and the hanger re-pressurized . . ."	• "When you're done ..."
• "We'll start with the assumption that Randy performed the preflight checks according to protocol."	• "We'll start with the assumption that Randy did the preflight checks correctly."

This:	**Became:**
• "Listening to you evaluate and summarize the options, my conclusion is that it boils down to air."	• "Based on your evaluation, it boils down to air."
• "He'll scrutinize our systems and procedures."	• "He'll audit everything."
• "It's a pretty long list, longer than I expected."	• "The list is longer than I expected."

Eliminate expressions that don't carry meaning, such as:

"Well, …"	"Aw, geez."
"Hey!"	"Oh my gosh."
"Um, …"	"Right?"

Phrases like these make dialogue sound rambley and unimportant. They reduce tension. These types of expressions can be useful as identifying lines, but use only one per character and use it sparingly.

If you struggle with dialogue compression, eliminate to-be verbs, as-ing sentence structure, *not* and *n't*, unnecessary uses of the word *that*, adverbs, adjectives, unnecessary preposition phrases, and wordiness, as discussed in Chapter 11.

Non-*said* Attributives

Attributives tell the reader who is speaking:

He said.
She said.
Mark said.
Mary said.
The cab driver said.
A disembodied voice said.

Avoid non-*said* attributives. These are words like *remarked, exclaimed, announced, asked, answered, inquired, muttered, cried out, replied, argued,* and others that tell the reader who's speaking. *Said* is invisible. Other words draw attention to the dialogue tag. What's more, they often contain redundant information. If the dialogue ends with an exclamation point, *exclaimed* is redundant. If it ends with a question mark, *asked* or *inquired* is redundant. If the character is responding to a question, *answered* is redundant. Others, like *announced* or *argued,* are shown by the content of the dialogue.

Choked, grunted, growled, and similar words are particularly bad because they aren't forms of speaking. It's physically impossible to choke, grunt, or growl a phrase.

When you must use an attributive, use *said* the overwhelming majority of the time.

Verb-first Attributives
Consider the following:

"It's over there," said she.

"It's over there," she said.

The former employs a verb-first attributive — the verb *said* comes before the name, noun, or pronoun used to identify the speaker. The latter seems more natural. It's the form readers are used to. Avoid verb-first attributives.

Dialogue, Actions, and Emotion
Consider the following passage:

Jorge slammed his fist on the table. "Well, you know, I really don't think that's such a good idea."

If the speaker's words are inconsistent with his actions, the reader won't believe whatever emotion you're trying to show. Your character's dialogue must match his actions and emotions:

> Jorge slammed his fist on the table. "Over my dead body."

This is better, but it's clichéd. How about:

> Jorge slammed his fist on the table. "Over my cold carcass."

Vocabulary
Edit long words out of your dialogue unless they're right for the character. Don't have her say:

> "Acquire the container."

People don't talk like that. Have her say:

> "Get the box."

This principle applies to your narrative as well.

Contractions
Use contractions wherever possible. Otherwise your dialogue will sound clunky and mechanical:

> "**We will** need results on this one," Snider told Chase. "And **we will** need them fast."
> "**I will** do what I can."
> "**That is** not good enough."

Contractions make dialogue more natural:

> "**We'll** need results on this one," Snider told Chase. "And
> **we'll** need them fast."
> "**I'll** do what I can."
> "**That's** not good enough."

The same rule applies to narrative.

Run-on Sentences and Sentence Fragments

Consider the following passage:

> "Have you had lunch?"
> "No, not yet."
> "Do you want to go to Stuffy's?"
> "That sounds good."

People don't generally speak in complete, grammatically correct sentences. Look for opportunities to make run-on sentences or to use sentence fragments to emulate speech patterns:

> "Had lunch?"
> "Not yet."
> "Stuffy's?"
> "Sounds good."

This comes back to compression. It not only makes your dialogue more natural, it makes it more crisp. It quickens the pace.

Melodramatic Dialogue

When dialogue is more dramatic than the scene warrants or when a writer tries to use dialogue as the primary vehicle to communicate the drama of the story, melodramatic dialogue results. This makes the dialogue ring false, as in the following example from a critique submission:

An hour later, [Jason] found himself in front of an old brick house. He marched up the front yard to the door, squashing a few azaleas as he went.

"Oy! Dominic! It's me!"

"I'm not home!" a deep voice came from behind the door. Jason noticed a hand ripping shut the curtains in a window.

"I'm not stupid, Dominic, let me in!"

Jason heard a short bark of laughter. "'I'm not stupid', he says! Hah! That's a good one. Now go away, I'm not here!"

"Dominic, open the blasted door before I break it down!"

The door opened. A tall, dark-haired man stood in the doorway, glaring down at Jason. "You interrupted my reading," he said. "I was at a good part."

"Yeah, well, too bad so sad. Let me in."

Dominic sighed and rolled his eyes, unlatching the screen door. "Fine. What do you want?" he grumbled as Jason pushed past him towards the kitchen.

"Food."

It's not clear if there's genuine animosity between these characters or just annoyance on the part of Dominic. If animosity, the author never reveals its source. Therefore, the dialogue seems overly dramatic for the situation. It must be toned down. Start by eliminating the exclamation points, direct address, and name-calling:

An hour later, [Jason] marched up the front yard to Dominic's old brick house, squashing azaleas as he went. He pounded on the door. "Open up. It's me."

"I'm not home." Dominic's deep voice came from beyond the door.

"Let me in. I need a favor."

"That's supposed to be incentive?" Nevertheless, Dominic opened the door. "You're interrupting my reading."

"Too bad." Jason pushed past him towards the kitchen. "I need food."

As a side note, I love the specificity in the first paragraph. Not just a house, but an old brick house. Not just flowers, but azaleas. I did, however, tighten the author's wording.

Look for melodrama anywhere your dialogue seems unnatural (to you or to somebody else) and rewrite the offending passages.

Dialect

I mentioned during character development (Chapter 2) that you should give each character a different manner of speaking. Dialect is one way to do this. People from different age groups, regions, countries, cultures, socioeconomic backgrounds, levels of education, time periods, and even genders speak differently. Beginning writers often use phonetic spelling to indicate the pronunciation of the accent or dialect they're trying to emulate. They create butchered words, like "Ohm'gosh," that look more like a vanity license plate than like a bit of dialogue. These are difficult for your reader to decipher. Instead, tell the reader your character speaks with an accent. If you remind him occasionally, he'll hear it as he reads the character's words.

If you decide to use phonetic spelling to show dialect or as an identifying line for one of your characters, use it sparingly. A little of this will go a long way.

Even simple devices, such as *c'mon*, *'bout*, *'em*, and *runnin'* are unnecessary. They look more colloquial than *come on*, *about*, *them*, and *running*, but to the reader, they're identical, so use the latter.

Gonna and *wanna* are clichés. Avoid them at all costs. Replace *wanna* with *want to*. You can often eliminate *gonna* without resorting to the more verbose and sometimes cumbersome *going to:*

This:	Becomes:
• "We're gonna have to shut them down."	• "We'll have to shut them down."
• "You gonna arrest me for it?"	• "You want to arrest me for it?"
• "That's not gonna happen."	• "That won't happen."

Study the language of the regional population you need to emulate. If possible, go where the people are and listen to them talk. Interview somebody from the group of interest. At a minimum, study their diction on the Internet.

Achieve dialect through word choice rather than through word-butchering. Consider the following lines. As you read each line, visualize the speaking character. What age group, geographic region, country, culture, socioeconomic background, level of education, time period, and gender does the character belong to?

"I aim to kill the varmint."
"He don't like me none."
"Verily I say unto you ..."
"Is he not wonderful?"
"Have you tea?"
"You're such a dork."

None of these lines is over six words long. Yet in each, word choice shows much about the character without resorting to phonetic spelling to illustrate his or her accent or pronunciation.

Some regional populations use a different lexicon from others'. A character from England, for example, might say *sweets* for *candy*, *nappy* for *diaper*, *chemist's* for *drug store*, *jersey* for *sweater*, and *waistcoat* for *vest*.

You get the idea.

Paragraph Breaks

Never put the dialogue of one character in the same paragraph with the actions of another. When writing dialogue, give each character his own paragraph. Doing so will help your reader keep track of who's doing the talking.

Consider this example from *Worlds Asunder*:

> Brower examined the display. His short, muscular body seemed to radiate confidence. "What's that marker just north-northwest of the **Phoenix**?" Snider asked. "Checking on that now, sir," Chavez said. But Robinson was faster. "That's a geological research base. Chinese. Fairly new. Just a couple of habitation tents."

This paragraph mentions four characters (Brower, Snider, Chavez, and Robinson) and contains three lines of dialogue. It takes a fair amount of deciphering to figure out who's saying what. If I divide the excerpt into paragraphs by speaker, I can make the dialogue much clearer without changing a single word of the passage:

> Brower examined the display. His short, muscular body seemed to radiate confidence.
>
> "What's that marker just north-northwest of the **Phoenix**?" Snider asked.
>
> "Checking on that now, sir," Chavez said.
>
> But Robinson was faster. "That's a geological research base. Chinese. Fairly new. Just a couple of habitation tents."

Dialogue Tags

Consider the placement of each dialogue tag. Don't place an attributive at the beginning of a sentence:

> **Chase said,** "Nevertheless, a lot of things went on in this cabin that I don't understand. If we explain one of them, it'll be worth our time."

Remember, attributives are supposed to be invisible. Placing one at the beginning of a sentence will draw attention to it.

If the dialogue line is more than a few words long, don't withhold the attributive until the end:

> "Nevertheless, a lot of things went on in this cabin that I don't understand. If we explain one of them, it'll be worth our time," **Chase said.**

Usually, the reader needs to know who's speaking in order for the dialogue to make sense within the context of the story. If you withhold the attributive, you may force the reader to go back and reread the dialogue once he knows who's talking.

Instead, insert the attributive at the first natural break in the rhythm of the dialogue (usually after the first comma or period):

> "Nevertheless," **Chase said,** "a lot of things went on in this cabin that I don't understand. If we explain one of them, it'll be worth our time."

This tells the reader who's talking early in the speech without conspicuously placing the attributive at the beginning of the sentence.

Now read your dialogue for too many tags, too few tags, or repetitive tags. Consider the following passage, which I've bastardized from a meeting scene in *Worlds Asunder* for the purpose of this example:

> "Did you search his quarters?"
> "Chief Brower may have. Frank and I were busy talking to Forsythe's neighbors and anyone else who lives or works between his place and the hangar."
> "Yeah, I took a look."
> "And?"
> "Things were in disarray."

"Signs of a struggle, you think?"
"No. It looked more like someone was looking for something."
"Any idea what?"
"No."

This example has too few dialogue tags. In fact, there are none. With three people in this conversation, the reader can't tell who's speaking. On the other hand, it's rarely necessary to provide an attributive for every dialogue line:

"Did you search his quarters?" **Chase asked Mike.**

"Chief Brower may have," **Mike said.** "Frank and I were busy talking to Forsythe's neighbors and anyone else who lives or works between his place and the hangar."

"Yeah, I took a look," **Brower said.**

"And?" **Chase asked.**

"Things were in disarray," **Brower replied.**

"Signs of a struggle, you think?" **Chase asked.**

"No," **Brower said.** "It looked more like someone was looking for something."

"Any idea what?" **Chase said.**

"No," **Brower replied.**

This passage contains so many attributives they become repetitive and cumbersome. What if I use beats — actions performed by the speaker — to disrupt the monotony?

Chase turned toward Mike. "Did you search his quarters?"

"Chief Brower may have." **Mike gestured to Brower.** "Frank and I were busy talking to Forsythe's neighbors and anyone else who lives or works between his place and the hangar."

Chase shifted his gaze.

Brower pulled his attention from the window and looked at Chase. "Yeah, I took a look."

Chase leaned forward. "And?"

Brower shrugged. "Things were in disarray."

Chase took a sip of his coffee and set the cup on the table. "Signs of a struggle, you think?"

"No." **Brower pursed his lips.** "It looked more like someone was looking for something."

Chase scowled. "Any idea what?"

Brower shook his head.

This is less repetitive than a string of attributives, but when you attach a beat to every line, it slows the pace of the conversation. This passage is supposed to come across as a brisk exchange. That feeling is lost in the example above.

So what's the answer? Don't use beats or attributives unless they're necessary to show character emotion, *essential* character action, or to identify the speaker. If it's clear who's speaking, let the dialogue stand alone. When you must identify the speaker, favor beats over attributives. Use them to reveal character and setting. If your beats began to clutter the dialogue, replace some with attributives to increase the pace.

The following passage shows this scene as it appears in *Worlds Asunder.*

"Did you search his quarters?" **Chase asked Mike.**

"Chief Brower may have. Frank and I were busy talking to Forsythe's neighbors and anyone else who lives or works between his place and the hangar."

Chase shifted his gaze.

"Yeah, I took a look," **Brower said.**

"And?"

"Things were in disarray."

"Signs of a struggle, you think?"

"No." He pursed his lips. "It looked more like someone was looking for something."

"Any idea what?"

Brower shook his head.

Let's look, line by line, at how I arrived at this solution.

I don't care for *looking* and *turning* beats (see Filter Words in Chapter 11), so I used an attributive in the first line.

The second line can stand alone. Chase asked Mike a question. Unless I indicate otherwise, the reader will assume Mike is the responding character.

Next, I show Chase shifting his gaze. This character action is essential to show he's addressing Stan Brower rather than Mike Penick. Alternatively, Chase could have said, "Stan?" but I thought it more natural for him to shift his attention with a gesture rather than with a spoken word.

As I enter the terse part of the dialogue, I use the simple attributive "Brower said" to establish him as the next speaker, and then launch into a ping-pong exchange. No tags are needed as long as Chase and Brower trade lines.

Near the end, I slow the pace with a beat:

He pursed his lips.

This doesn't actually tell the reader who's speaking. I added it strictly to show Brower's careful consideration of Chase's question.

Finally, I replaced the last line with:

Brower shook his head.

I felt this was more realistic than the oral response. Furthermore, closing the exchange with a silent gesture helped smooth the transition into the next part of the scene.

The lesson to learn from this brief example is: When it comes to dialogue tags, balance and pacing are key. When you think you're done, read your dialogue out loud. Doing so is the only way to determine if you've struck the right balance.

Explanatory Tags

Eliminate beats and attributives that explain dialogue content:

> Chase crossed the room to Brower. **He had to find out what was happening, and he suspected that Brower would know**. "What's going on, Stan? What's with the spooks?"

Is the dialogue any less clear in the following passage?

> Chase crossed the room to Brower. "What's going on, Stan? What's with the spooks?"

When you feel the need to explain your dialogue, it means the passage is unclear, you're patronizing your reader, or both. Furthermore, it demonstrates a lack of self-confidence. If you've written the dialogue well, the reader will understand it. If not, revise the dialogue rather than explaining it.

When you're not sure if the dialogue is clear, err on the side of subtlety. Your critiquer will tell you if it doesn't make sense. See Chapter 15 for more on critiques.

Tags that Tell Emotion

Read through your dialogue and look specifically for tags that tell emotion, as in the example below:

> "Herrera was on board."
> "On the *Phoenix*?" Chase said, **surprised**. "What was he doing there?"

You may have shown the emotion well enough through the actions, thoughts, and dialogue of the character. If you haven't, use the techniques discussed in "Showing Emotions" (Chapter 9) to show the emotion. Either way, delete the part of the tag that tells emotion.

Below, I offer three ways to correct the passage above. I show Chase's surprise through his actions, thoughts, and dialogue, respectively:

> "On the *Phoenix*?" **Chase glanced at the central hologram, as if it could somehow confirm the news.** "What was he doing there?"

> "On the *Phoenix*?" *He couldn't be.* "What was he doing there?"

> "On the *Phoenix*?" Chase said. "What **the hell** was he doing there?"

Punctuation

Writers make a variety of mistakes in dialogue punctuation. Follow the rules below to avoid the errors I most commonly see in critique submissions.

1 Em-dash (—)

An em-dash indicates an interruption of the speaker.

2 Ellipsis (...)

An ellipsis shows the speaker trailing off.

3 Exclamation point (!)

Reserve exclamation points for when your character is genuinely shouting. Never use multiple exclamation points. If you use them sparingly, one will provide the necessary emphasis.

4   Uppercase words
     Don't use uppercase text to show emphasis. If you must supply emphasis, use italics, but do so sparingly. Whenever possible, reword the dialogue to make the speaker's meaning clear without changing the style of the text.

5   Semicolon (;)
     Don't use a semicolon in dialogue. Choose a comma or period. Use sentence fragments and run-on sentences to emulate natural speech patterns.

6   Exclaimed questions (?!)
     Never use a question mark and an exclamation point at the end of the same sentence. If it's a question, use a question mark. If it's a shouted question, follow it with, "he shouted." This is an exception to the non-*said* attributive rule.

Sound and Pacing

Read your dialogue scene out loud for sound and pacing. Does it sound natural? Does it have the rhythm of speech? Is it tense and engaging? Have you achieved the desired pace?

Exercises

1 Select a dialogue scene you've written. Replace every attributive, including *said*, with a beat (an action performed by the speaker). Don't fall back on crutch devices, like having your character turn or glance at the person he's addressing. Choose beats that do at least one of the following: 1) show an emotion, 2) show a setting element that is different from the reader's here-and-now, or 3) show an identifying prop or mannerism of the speaking character. These kinds of beats bring your story and characters to life. While it's unnecessary, even detrimental, to replace every attributive in your writing, this exercise will provide practice in generating effective beats.

2 Go back to the original scene from Exercise 1. Change all of the attributives to *said* and delete dialogue tags that tell, rather than show, emotion. Delete tags that explain the dialogue content. Now read the revised scene. Does this scene lack any information or emotion that existed in the original version? If so, show the information or emotion without using non-*said*, emotion-telling, or explanatory attributives. (Hint: Use some of the beats you created in Exercise 1). Have someone read both versions of the scene. Ask the reader which she liked better and why.

3 Select a dialogue scene you've written, possibly the revised scene from Exercise 2. Cut every line of dialogue down to five or fewer words. Use contractions and fragmented sentences as necessary to emulate realistic speech. If you can't convey the entire meaning or intent of the line in five words, convey only the most important part of the meaning or intent.

Read the revised scene out loud. Is the compressed dialogue punchier? Does it convey a faster pace? Does it carry more tension? Does it seem more natural? The answer to these questions is often yes, but not always. Keep the compressed lines that work. For those that don't, revert to the original or choose an intermediate solution. Have someone read both version of the scene. Ask the reader which he liked better and why.

13

Case Studies

The changes discussed in Chapters 11 and 12 may seem subtle, but they will have a powerful cumulative effect on the quality of your writing, as illustrated by these extended examples.

Case Study 1

> Nothing had changed from the day before. The clearing was empty and the tall stalks of sugarcane that guarded [Antonio] were quiet. What had waked him? Something had to be out there. But what? Or who?
>
> Antonio cocked his head to listen for any strange sounds. Nothing. Had someone crunched through the cane fields and gone on? Or were they still out there, watching and waiting. A wave of terror swept through him. He swallowed hard. His Papá had left him in charge so it was up to him to find out if anyone else was in the cane field. It was not always easy to be the only son of a Mexican hidalgo, he thought, even when he was in Texas.

This passage, excerpted from a critique submission, suffers from several problems. I'll discuss and correct each in turn.

▌ Show and tell

The excerpt is too short to evaluate for many of the scene problems from Chapter 9. We can look for *tell*, however, in even the briefest passages. The following sentence *tells*:

> Something had to be out there.

The author could omit this sentence entirely. From the context, it's obvious something's out there. If she wants the reader to know Antonio's thinking this, however, she could show Antonio responding to the thought:

> Antonio listened for the source of the sound that had awakened him.

Here's another case of *tell*:

> A wave of terror swept through him.

How does Antonio (or his body) react to his terror?

> A chill crept up his spine despite the warm air.

Notice that I've also worked a setting detail (warm air) into the action of the scene.

Finally:

> His Papá had left him in charge so it was up to him to find out if anyone else was in the cane field.

This isn't *tell* in the strict sense of drawing a conclusion for the reader. It's more a case of stopping the action to provide backstory. Nevertheless, remedy it in the same way:

Oh, Papa, I'm only ten, why did you leave me in charge?

Here I've worked in Antonio's age, which is important. If the reader knows how old Antonio is, she can better understand his danger. A fifteen-year-old, for instance, could handle trouble much more readily than a ten-year-old could. As for the rest, let the reader conclude that Antonio must solve his own problem.

2   Questions in a character's thoughts

Look at the questions that appear in Antonio's thoughts:

> What had waked him?
>
> But what?
>
> Or who?
>
> Had someone crunched through the cane fields and gone on?
>
> Or were they still out there, watching and waiting?

None of these sentences is necessary. The reader will wonder these things without the author having to ask.

Now, I know what you're thinking. As part of correcting *tell*, I added a question in Antonio's thoughts:

Oh, Papa, I'm only ten. Why did you leave me in charge?

This question is different from the one the reader should ask herself. The reader should wonder what's out there and if it's going to get Antonio. At the moment, why his father left is secondary. This is a subtle but important distinction. It's okay for your character to ask himself a question but not for you, as the author, to pose a question to your reader.

3   To-be verbs

The passage now contains five to-be verbs:

> Nothing had changed from the day before. The clearing **was** empty and the tall stalks of sugarcane that guarded him **were** quiet. Antonio listened for the source of the sound that had awakened him.
>
> Antonio cocked his head to listen for any strange sounds. Nothing. A chill crept up his spine despite the warm air. He swallowed hard. *Oh, Papa, I'm only ten, why did you leave me in charge?* It **was** not always easy **to be** the only son of a Mexican hidalgo, he thought, even when he **was** in Texas.

All the to-be verbs are in either the second sentence or the last sentence. Let's look at them one sentence at a time:

> The clearing **was** empty and the tall stalks of sugarcane that guarded him **were** quiet.

This can be rewritten without the to-be verbs:

> The tall stalks of sugarcane remained silent sentinels over the empty clearing.

Despite the to-be verbs, I like the first half of the final sentence:

> It **was** not always easy **to be** the only son of a Mexican hidalgo …

This elegantly works a character detail into Antonio's thoughts, worded the way he would probably say it if he were speaking aloud. Therefore, I'd leave this phrase alone. The second half of the sentence is a different story:

> ... even when he **was** in Texas.

This is here solely to reveal Antonio's location. It's important to let the reader know where the story takes place, but this can be done more smoothly by adding the word *Texas* to my rewrite of the second sentence:

> The tall stalks of Texas sugarcane remained silent sentinels over the empty clearing.

Putting it all together

> Nothing had changed from the day before. The tall stalks of Texas sugarcane remained silent sentinels over the empty clearing. **Antonio listened for the source of the sound that had awakened him.**
> **Antonio cocked his head to listen for any strange sounds.** Nothing. A chill crept up his spine despite the warm air and he swallowed hard. *Oh, Papa, I'm only ten. Why did you leave me in charge?* It was not always easy to be the only son of a Mexican hidalgo.

Always go back and re-read your revised passage, preferably out loud. Here, the first sentence of the second paragraph repeats the preceding sentence. We need to eliminate one or the other. I like the specificity at the end of the first paragraph; it conveys what Antonio's listening for. I also like the character action that begins the second paragraph:

Antonio cocked his head ...

Therefore, I'd combine the best elements of both:

Nothing had changed from the day before. The tall stalks of Texas sugarcane remained silent sentinels over the empty clearing.

Antonio cocked his head and listened for the source of the sound that had awakened him. Nothing. A chill crept up his spine despite the warm air and he swallowed hard. *Oh, Papa, I'm only ten. Why did you leave me in charge?* It was not always easy to be the only son of a Mexican hidalgo.

Compare this with the original text and decide for yourself which is more compelling to read.

Case Study 2

The following example is a dream scene from the beginning of a critique submission. Because it's a dream, it will appear in italic text in the manuscript. Plain text is easier to read, however, so that's what I've used here.

Kari wandered mindlessly through the forest. The black clouds above blocked any light that tried to seep through. A gentle gurgle drew her toward the small stream she knew lay ahead beside the trail. A figure clothed in black sat beside the stream, letting his pale fingers linger in the slow moving water. His black hair fell lazily onto his forehead, and his golden brown eyes wandered from ripple to ripple. She moved toward him in a trance-like state, intrigued and slightly scared. A cold wind pushed against her, licking her face with icy tentacles. She ignored it and continued forward. She stumbled on a rock and fell, landing in front of him.

He started and stared at her. "You should not be here. It is impermissible," came his smooth voice with perceptible deadliness. His white teeth glittered in the bright moonlight that broke out from the clouds above.

Kari gasped when she saw fangs.

"Leave," he ordered, standing. He was five foot ten and skinny, but muscles rippled under his skin, flaunting strength. He reached down and picked her up. Spinning around, he threw her toward the river.

This is a pretty polished piece of writing. I've included it here to demonstrate that the techniques discussed in this book can improve even well-written fiction.

1 Point of view

This passage contains one subtle viewpoint violation:

He was **five foot ten** and skinny.

Unless the viewpoint character has a tape measure or knows from some other experience exactly how tall the figure is, she can't be sure of his height to this degree of precision. The author could write:

He was **about five foot ten** and skinny.

I would opt for a less verbose option:

He was **tall** and skinny.

This captures the impression I believe the author is trying to convey better than an exact height does. If the reader perceives the figure to be tall, the description of him as skinny will have more impact.

2   To-be verbs

> "You should not **be** here. It **is** impermissible."

This is an awkward line of dialogue. Besides including two to-be verbs, the author chose *should not* over the contraction *shouldn't*. The awkwardness, however, is deliberate. It represents the style of speech the author has chosen for this character. She refers back to this trait in a later scene. As such, this is a clear case of breaking the rules to achieve a specific effect. I applaud it.

This passage contains another to-be verb, however, that should be eliminated:

> He **was** five foot ten and skinny, but muscles rippled under his skin, flaunting strength.

Or with the revision I suggested earlier:

> He **was** tall and skinny, but muscles rippled under his skin, flaunting strength.

I would rewrite this as:

> Muscles rippled under the skin of his tall, lanky body, flaunting strength.

I changed *skinny* to *lanky* to avoid using two forms of the word *skin* in the same sentence.

3   As-ing sentences

> She stumbled on a rock and fell, land**ing** in front of him.

becomes:

> She stumbled on a rock, fell, and landed in front of
> him.

or just:

> She stumbled on a rock and fell in front of him.

In the following example, the first sentence is wordy, and the second is an as-ing sentence:

> He reached down and picked her up. Spin**ning**
> around, he threw her toward the river.

These sentences can be revised:

> He picked her up, spun around, and threw her to-
> ward the water.

Here's another example:

> "Leave," he ordered, stand**ing**.

This combined beat and attributive can be rewritten:

> "Leave." He stood.

The author can make it more dramatic with some dark imagery:

> "Leave." The figure stood and thrust his pale finger
> toward the trail.

This also emphasizes that this is a command without saying, "he ordered." I changed *he* to *the figure* to avoid a repeated sentence beginning — the next sentence also starts with *he*.

What about the following as-ing sentence?

> Muscles rippled under the skin of his tall, lanky body, flaunt**ing** strength.

I would leave this one alone. The figure's muscles are, in fact, rippling and flaunting simultaneously, as implied by the as-ing structure. Furthermore, I think the wording is smoother than the altered form:

> Muscles rippled under the skin of his tall, lanky body and flaunted strength.

Read both versions of this sentence out loud and decide for yourself which has an easier rhythm. I would leave the remaining as-ing sentence unaltered for similar reasons:

> A figure clothed in black sat beside the stream, let-t**ing** his pale fingers linger in the slow moving water.

4   Repeated words

In this dream scene, the writer has occasionally used repeated sentence beginnings and other repeated words. Look at the second and third sentences of the first paragraph:

> **A** gentle gurgle drew her toward the small **stream** she knew lay ahead beside the trail. **A** figure clothed in black sat beside the **stream**, letting his pale fingers linger in the slow moving water.

Here, the author uses the word *a* to begin two consecutive sentences. She repeats *stream* in the same two sentences. Restructure the passage to avoid the repeats:

> The gentle gurgle of a small **brook** drew her ahead. A figure, clothed in black, sat beside the **stream**, letting his pale fingers linger in the slowly moving water.

In this revision, I also corrected a minor grammatical error. The water is *slowly* moving, not *slow* moving.

The author also used the word *wandered* twice in the first paragraph. I would replace one with a synonym:

> ... his golden brown eyes roamed from ripple to ripple.

Finally, the original passage contained a repeated sentence beginning, *he*, in the last paragraph, which I corrected when I eliminated the to-be verb from this paragraph.

5   Verb choice and comparisons

In most of these case studies, I've refrained from commenting on the strengths of the passage, preferring to focus on how to correct the weaknesses. Nevertheless, the verb choice and comparisons in this example deserve acknowledgement:

> A cold wind **pushed** against her, licking her face with **icy tentacles**.

The imagery in sentences like this account for much of the scene's effectiveness, even prior to the minor wording changes I've made along the way.

6   Adverbs

As noted above, the author has done a great job selecting many of her verbs. Nevertheless, adverbs indicate opportunities for improvement.

This:	Could become:
• **slowly** moving	• meandering or ambling
• fell **lazily** onto	• fell onto, draped over or stroked
• **slightly** scared	• nervous, anxious, or intimidated

I would leave *mindlessly* in the opening sentence. It adds meaning that's difficult to convey without the adverb.

7   Dialogue

I see only one dialogue problem:

> He started and stared at her. "You should not be here. It is impermissible," came his smooth voice with perceptible deadliness. His white teeth glittered in the bright moonlight that broke out from the clouds above.
> Kari gasped when she saw fangs.

Consider this attributive from the passage above:

> ... came his smooth voice with perceptible deadliness.

This attributive is made unnecessary by the beats contained in the same paragraph. Furthermore, the quality of the figure's voice can be included more smoothly as a beat:

He started and stared at her. "You should not be here." **His smooth voice carried a perceptible deadliness.** "It is impermissible."

Kari gasped when she saw his white fangs glitter in the bright moonlight that broke out from the clouds above.

I reworded the last sentence to avoid beginning two sentences in the same paragraph with *his*.

8 Putting it all together

Again, the changes are subtle, yet the revised passage below is notably tighter than the original passage. Compare them for yourself:

Kari wandered mindlessly through the forest. The black clouds above blocked any light that tried to seep through. The gentle gurgle of a small brook drew her ahead. A figure, clothed in black, sat beside the stream, and his pale fingers lingered in the ambling water. His black hair stroked his forehead and his golden brown eyes roamed from ripple to ripple. She moved toward him in a trance-like state, intrigued and anxious. A cold wind pushed against her. It licked her face with icy tentacles, but she ignored it and continued forward. She stumbled on a rock and fell in front of him.

He started and stared at her. "You should not be here." His smooth voice carried a perceptible deadliness. "It is impermissible."

Kari gasped when she saw his white fangs glitter in the bright moonlight that broke out from the clouds above.

"Leave." The figure stood and thrust his pale finger toward the trail. Muscles rippled under the skin of his tall, lanky body, flaunting strength.

He picked her up, spun around, and threw her toward the water.

Case Study 3

The following excerpt was taken from the early-draft critique submission in which the opening paragraph shows the vampire, Jason, entering a club filled with unsuspecting teenagers. I selected this passage for two reasons. First, it offers an opportunity to improve faulty dialogue. Second, it will show the importance of characterization in establishing tension and suspense.

[Jason] finally spotted a likely prospect: two girls sitting together, reapplying their gothic makeup and talking on their cell phones. He grinned. He would have no problem getting one of them alone.

"What can I get for you tonight, sir?" a voice asked, snapping him out of his thoughts.

"How 'bout a Coke?" Jason said, not really thirsty.

"All right, I'll be just a moment ..."

Jason sipped his drink coolly, keeping an eye on the two girls the whole time until one of them left for the bathroom. This was his chance. He stood up and sauntered over to the other girl, who was now off her phone and was twirling her red hair around it while she chewed on a jet-black fingernail.

"Excuse me," he said over the music. The girl looked up.

"Hey."

"What's your name?"

"Susan."

"Susan. What a pretty name. You alone?" Jason asked, although he already knew the answer to that.

"Naw," Susan said. "I'm waiting for my friend; she's in the bathroom."

"I see. Well, would you like to step outside with me for a minute?" **Yes. Say yes.**

"Yes," Susan said, as if on cue. "Lemme go tell my friend where I am, 'kay?"

Jason nodded, and Susan walked over to the bathroom, sticking her head inside and shouting, "Hey, Mindy! I'm gonna go outside for a minute, all right?"

Jason thought he heard the other girl call out, "Huh?" but Susan had already turned away and started heading for the front door.

"Let's go."

I'll apply the scene-editing techniques from Chapter 9 before moving into prose and dialogue.

1   Show and tell

"You alone?" Jason asked, **although he already knew the answer to that.**

In this line, everything after the comma is *tell*. The author has already shown that the girl's not alone and that Jason knows it. If you've both shown and told something, leave the part that shows and delete the part that tells:

"You alone?" Jason asked.

Similarly, delete the following sentence:

This was his chance.

It's clear from the context that this is Jason's chance.

2　Point of view

Two phrases catch my eye when I consider the viewpoint of this passage:

> He grinned.

Jason can't see himself grinning, so this sentence is a viewpoint violation. My real concern, however, rests much more deeply than with what Jason can or can't see.

In this story, Jason is the protagonist. Because he is a vampire, the reader will need a compelling reason to like, or at least understand, him. "He grinned" suggests Jason enjoys the consumption of human blood and maybe even the thrill of murder. If so, the author will have to work hard to give the reader something he can relate to in the Jason character. Even so, "he grinned" is a nebulous, even lazy, way to describe Jason's pleasure. Instead, show what that pleasure feels like from Jason's perspective.

If Jason feeds purely out of necessity, "he grinned" is inappropriate and misleading. I'm unsure of the author's intent, but for the sake of this example I'll assume the latter and delete the sentence.

The other viewpoint problem is Jason's line:

> "Susan. What a pretty name ..."

I would delete this line as well. Because Jason plans to use his mind tricks to force Susan's compliance, he doesn't need to flatter her. Furthermore, he doesn't have time. Susan's friend could return at any moment.

3　Building tension

I see two easy opportunities to increase tension. First, delete:

> **He would have no problem** getting one of them alone.

This makes Jason's task easy. Never make anything easy, especially for your protagonist. Instead, state it as a problem:

> **He had to** get one of them alone.

The author could go a step further and have some other guy get to Susan first. Doing so will give Jason an additional obstacle, one that will force him to interact with other characters (always a good thing) and will make the reader believe, if only briefly, that Susan might be saved.

The other tension-building opportunity is subtler:

> ... until one of them left for the bathroom.

In this sentence, *them* refers to Jason's prospects. When one goes to the bathroom, the other becomes Jason's victim. The author can make this ominously clear:

> ... until one, **the lucky one**, left for the bathroom.

Now let's look at the prose.

4 To-be verbs

Four out of seven to-be verbs appear within spoken lines of dialogue. These will take care of themselves as we address dialogue. I removed one of the others when I eliminated *tell*. Two remain:

> He stood up and sauntered over to the other girl, who **was** now off her phone and **was** twirling her

red hair around it while she chewed on a jet-black fingernail.

Delete the phrase, "who was now off her phone." It's a repeated element. If the girl is twirling her hair around her phone and chewing on her fingernail, then her phone, both hands, and her mouth are otherwise occupied. Obviously she's not still talking on the phone. Rewrite the rest of the sentence using past tense rather than using past progressive:

He stood up and sauntered over to the other girl, who twirled her red hair around her phone and chewed on a jet-black fingernail.

5   As-ing sentence structures
    Several of these appear in the passage:

He finally spotted a likely prospect: two girls sitting together, reapply**ing** their gothic makeup and talk-**ing** on their cell phones.

I'm skeptical that both girls are reapplying their makeup and talking on the phone simultaneously. For the sake of this example, I'll assume one is applying makeup and the other talking on the phone.

He finally spotted a likely prospect. Across the bar, two girls sat together, one reapply**ing** her gothic makeup and the other talk**ing** on her cell phone.

Notice that this still constitutes an as-ing structure, but now the actions of each girl (sitting and applying makeup, or sitting and talking on the phone) are, in fact, simultaneous. As such, the as-ing structure isn't harmful to the author's style.

Consider this as-ing sentence:

"What can I get for you tonight, sir?" a voice asked, snapp**ing** him out of his thoughts.

This is a combined beat and attributive. Keep the beat and delete the attributive:

"What can I get for you tonight, sir?" A voice snapped him out of his thoughts.

Here are some others:

Jason sipped his drink coolly, keep**ing** an eye on the two girls ...

Susan walked over to the bathroom, stick**ing** her head inside and shout**ing** ...

Rewrite these without the as-ing structure:

Jason sipped his drink coolly and kept an eye on the two girls ...

Susan walked over to the bathroom, stuck her head inside, and shouted ...

6   Filter words and thinker attributives
We've already eliminated the thinker attributive in:

... he already **knew** the answer to that.

There's a filter word and a thinker attributive in:

Jason **thought** he **heard** the other girl call out ...

Rewrite this as:

> The other girl called out.

7 Specificity

> **A voice** snapped him out of his thoughts.

Not just a voice, but the bartender's voice:

> **The bartender's voice** snapped him out of his thoughts.

8 Repeated elements

> Jason sipped his drink coolly and kept an eye on the **two** girls the whole time **until** one of them left for the bathroom.

This sentence has two repeated elements. The first is the word *two*. The reader already knows there're two girls, so the author doesn't have to say it again. Also, the word *until* implies "the whole time." I'd delete the latter:

> Jason sipped his drink coolly and kept an eye on the girls until one of them left for the bathroom.

9 Adverbs

> Jason **finally** spotted a **likely** prospect.

This sentence contains two unnecessary adverbs. Worse, the phrase *likely prospect* borders on cliché. Delete both adverbs.

Another appears in:

> Jason sipped his drink **coolly** and kept an eye on
> the girls ...

I could just delete the word *coolly*, but the author never showed the bartender delivering Jason's drink. He just went off to prepare it. Because the author hasn't accounted for the time between Jason's ordering the Coke and his drinking it, the transition between these two events feels awkward. I would avoid this by writing:

> Jason kept an eye on the girls ...

10 Wordiness

For now, I'll ignore dialogue and focus on tightening phrases in the narrative.

This:	**Becomes:**
• He stood up and sauntered over to the other girl . . .	• He sauntered over to the other girl . . .
• ... but Susan had already turned away and started heading for the front door.	• ... but Susan had already started for the door.

11 Clarity

> "... would you like to step outside with me for a
> minute?" *Yes. Say yes.*
> "Yes," Susan said, as if on cue.

It's clear that "Yes. Say yes" is in Jason's thoughts, but is it wishful thinking or some sort of telepathic command? From context, it appears to be the latter, but the phrase "*as if* on cue" implies it's not. This scene is written from Jason's point of view. If he gave her a cue, write:

"Yes," Susan said on cue.

From a characterization standpoint, if Susan's answer was forced upon her, she should be surprised by it:

"Yes," Susan said on cue, her face perplexed.

Alternatively, the author could make the mental command clear by writing:

"... would you like to step outside with me for a minute?" *Yes. Say yes,* Jason commanded.

That, however, wouldn't be very subtle.

12 Putting the prose edits together
Here's what we have so far:

[Jason] spotted a prospect. Across the bar, two girls sat together, one reapplying her gothic make-up, the other talking on her cell phone. He had to get one of them alone.

"What can I get for you tonight, sir?" The bartender's voice snapped him out of his thoughts.

"How 'bout a Coke?" Jason said, not really thirsty.

"All right, I'll be just a moment ...

Jason kept an eye on the girls until one, the lucky one, left for the bathroom. He sauntered over to the other girl, who twirled her red hair and chewed on a jet-black fingernail.

"Excuse me," he said over the music. The girl looked up.

"Hey."

"What's your name?"

"Susan."

"You alone?" Jason asked.

"Naw," Susan said. "I'm waiting for my friend; she's in the bathroom."

"I see. Well, would you like to step outside with me for a minute?" *Yes. Say yes.*

"Yes," Susan said on cue, her face perplexed. "Lemme go tell my friend where I am, 'kay?"

Jason nodded. She walked to the bathroom, stuck her head inside and shouted, "Hey, Mindy! I'm gonna go outside for a minute, all right?"

The other girl called out, "Huh?" but Susan had already started for the door.

"Let's go."

Improvement is already evident, but it's also clear that, no matter how polished the narrative passages are, a dialogue scene doesn't work without sharp dialogue.

13 Informative dialogue

When the bartender goes to get Jason's drink, he says:

"All right, **I'll be just a moment**."

Delete everything after the comma. Both Jason and the bartender know that even pouring a quick fountain drink isn't instantaneous. The reader knows it too.

14 Compression

Almost every dialogue line in this passage can benefit from compression.

This:	**Becomes:**
• "What can I get for you tonight, sir?"	• "What can I get you?"
• "How 'bout a Coke?"	• "Coke."

This:	**Becomes:**
• "I'm waiting for my friend; she's in the bathroom."	• "My friend's in the bathroom."
• "I see. Well, would you like to step outside with me for a minute?"	• "Would you like to step outside for a minute?"
• "Lemme go tell my friend where I am, 'kay?"	• "Let me tell my friend."
• "Hey, Mindy! I'm gonna go outside for a minute, all right?"	• "Hey, Mindy! I'm going outside for a minute."

I also corrected the dialect misspelling in the last two passages.

Finally:

"Huh?"

Sometimes the best way to compress dialogue is to delete it entirely, which I'd do with this line.

I cannot overstate the importance of dialogue compression. Compare the passage below with the one above and notice the difference compression can make:

[Jason] spotted a prospect. Across the bar, two girls sat together, one reapplying her gothic make-up, the other talking on her cell phone. He had to get one of them alone.

"What can I get you?" The bartender's voice snapped him out of his thoughts.

"Coke," Jason said, not really thirsty.

"All right."

Jason kept an eye on the girls until one, the lucky one, left for the bathroom. He sauntered over to the other girl, who twirled her red hair and chewed on a jet-black fingernail.

"Excuse me," he said over the music. The girl looked up.

"Hey."

"What's your name?"

"Susan."

"You alone?" Jason asked.

"Naw," Susan said. "My friend's in the bathroom."

"Would you like to step outside for a minute?" *Yes. Say yes.*

"Yes," Susan said on cue, her face perplexed. "Let me go tell my friend."

Jason nodded. She walked to the bathroom, stuck her head inside, and shouted, "Hey, Mindy! I'm going outside for a minute."

The other girl called out, but Susan had already started for the door.

"Let's go."

15 Non-*said* attributives

"You alone?" **Jason asked.**

Because Susan spoke the previous line, and because the author changed paragraphs, Jason's clearly speaking this line. The attributive is unnecessary. I'd delete it.

One non-*said* attributive remains:

She walked to the bathroom, stuck her head inside, and **shouted**, "Hey, Mindy! I'm going outside for a minute."

In this case, *shouted* communicates a volume appropriate to the setting. I'd keep it.

16 Paragraph breaks

> "Excuse me," he said over the music. The girl
> looked up.
> "Hey."
> "What's your name?"

The first paragraph of this passage contains Jason's dialogue and Susan's action. When writing dialogue, separate your paragraphs by character:

> "Excuse me," he said over the music.
> The girl looked up. "Hey."
> "What's your name?"

The same holds true for the following paragraph:

> Jason nodded. She walked to the bathroom, stuck
> her head inside, and shouted, "Hey, Mindy! I'm go-
> ing outside for a minute."

Corrected, this becomes:

> Jason nodded.
> She walked to the bathroom, stuck her head in-
> side, and shouted, "Hey, Mindy! I'm going outside
> for a minute."

17 Dialogue tags

Read the passage we have so far. Pay particular attention to the beats and attributives. Is it clear who's speaking each line of dialogue? Is the pace hampered by the beats? Are there too many attributes?

[Jason] spotted a prospect. Across the bar, two girls sat together, one reapplying her gothic make-up, the other talking on her cell phone. He had to get one of them alone.

"What can I get you?" **The bartender's voice snapped him out of his thoughts.**

"Coke," **Jason said,** not really thirsty.

"All right."

Jason kept an eye on the girls until one, the lucky one, left for the bathroom. He sauntered over to the other girl, who twirled her red hair and chewed on a jet-black fingernail. "Excuse me," **he said** over the music.

The girl looked up. "Hey."

"What's your name?"

"Susan."

"You alone?"

"Naw," **Susan said.** "My friend's in the bathroom."

"Would you like to step outside for a minute?" *Yes. Say yes.*

"Yes," **Susan said** on cue, her face perplexed. "Let me go tell my friend."

Jason nodded.

She walked to the bathroom, stuck her head inside, and **shouted**, "Hey, Mindy! I'm going outside for a minute."

The other girl called out, but Susan had already started for the door.

"Let's go."

Replacing *Susan* with the pronoun *she* in the following paragraph prevents unnecessary repetition of Susan's name in the dialogue tags.

"Naw," **Susan said**. "My friend's in the bathroom."

In the original passage, it's not clear who speaks the final line of dialogue. I'll assign it to Susan and provide a beat to identify her as the speaker:

She passed Jason without looking at him.
"Let's go."

18 Putting it all together

Jason spotted a prospect. Across the bar, two girls sat together, one reapplying her gothic make-up and the other talking on her cell phone.

"What can I get you?" The bartender's voice snapped him out of his thoughts.

"Coke," Jason said, not really thirsty.

"All right."

Jason kept an eye on the girls until one, the lucky one, left for the bathroom. He sauntered over to the other girl, who twirled her red hair and chewed on a jet-black fingernail. "Excuse me," he said over the music.

The girl looked up. "Hey."

"What's your name?"

"Susan."

"You alone?"

"Naw," she said. "My friend's in the bathroom."

"Would you like to step outside for a minute?" *Yes. Say yes.*

"Yes," Susan said on cue, her face perplexed. "Let me tell my friend." She walked to the bathroom, stuck her head inside, and shouted, "Hey, Mindy! I'm going outside for a minute."

The other girl called out, but Susan had already started for the door.

She passed Jason without looking at him. "Let's go."

Compare this with the original excerpt. The revision has more punch and realism, a faster pace, and a bit more tension. The ideas discussed under tension above would further improve it, yet it's still missing something.

Do you, the reader, care whether Jason feeds, whether he feeds on Susan, or whether it kills her?

No? Why not? Because you don't know enough about either character. For the sake of this example, I've handicapped the author by taking the passage out of context. As a result, you're missing any character background she might have provided. For example, does Jason intend to murder Susan or just drink enough blood to keep himself alive, leaving her weakened but unharmed? Does he feel any hesitation or guilt about having to do so? How did he become a vampire in the first place? Was he just a victim, as Susan is now?

These are the kinds of details that make the character real and give the scene the importance it needs to tug at your reader's heartstrings.

What if you knew Susan? What if you liked her? How would that affect the suspense as Jason leads her into the alley behind the club?

Suppose she takes care of her ailing mother and her young sister. *Suppose* her death would leave her family without a caregiver. How would that affect your emotional response to her peril? Even if you don't know her, if this is Susan's first appearance in the story, the author could establish these details from Jason's viewpoint by having him overhear a conversation between Susan and Mindy or between Susan and someone on the other end of her cell phone. How would that make Jason feel about choosing her as his victim? All these things would add depth to the characters and tension to the scene.

Don't underestimate the importance of characterization in creating effective tension and suspense.

Case Study 4

Now let's revisit the first case study from Chapter 10 to work on the prose and dialogue problems we left unaddressed. The final passage of that case study is repeated here for your convenience.

> Tama Fook and his brother, Greggis, crouched behind a large granite boulder jutting from the dry earth.
>
> "Hey, Tama Fook, did you see that? Frack. What **is** that?"
>
> "Quiet, Greggis!"
>
> "But that black mist just came out of the ground." Tama Fook saw part of the black mist rise up. Still as the dead, the air contained not a breath of wind. Nonetheless, the mist moved. Aimlessly at first, then it turned toward the brothers and the air grew cold.
>
> "Silence."
>
> Weeks of beard clung to Greggis' face in ragged, dust-clotted knots. Horror began to mask his expression. "It**'s** moving and there**'s** no wind. What do we do?"
>
> "Yes. I know it**'s** moving. We need to **be** quiet!" Tama Fook whispered, and then he hit his brother on the arm.
>
> They crouched down behind a rock as they watched the mist move to the northwest, this thing, whatever it **was**, they watched it moving really slow.
>
> "Should we follow it? Or should we go tell somebody what we saw?"
>
> "Well, I**'m** not following it, Greggis. And I**'m** not going back to Dusa City without the satchels."

Prose

The prose problems here are: to-be verbs, filter words, repeated elements, and a single unnecessary adverb.

The passage contains eight to-be verbs (shown in bold text above), including the ones buried in contractions. Seven of these appear in dialogue. Therefore I'll address them during the dialogue discussion below.

For now, consider the following sentences:

> Tama Fook **saw** part of the black mist rise up out of the ground.

> They crouched down behind a rock as they **watched** the mist move to the northwest, this thing, whatever it **was**, they **watched** it moving **really** slow.

These two passages contain all of the filter words, the remaining to-be verb, the unnecessary adverb, and no new information. Delete them both.

Doing so eliminates most of the repeated elements as well, but one remains. Five lines of dialogue include three cases of one character shushing the other:

> "Quiet, Greggis!"

> "Silence."

> "Yes. I know it**'s** moving. We need to **be** quiet!"

Eliminate two. The question is: Which two? This choice is largely a matter of taste. I'd keep the third. It occurs when the mist heads their way and after most of the conversation has taken place.

2 Informative dialogue

> "But that black mist just came out of the ground."

> "It's moving and there's no wind."

These lines serve only to inform the reader of events that both characters can see. By using dialogue to tell the reader about the mist, the author has lost the opportunity to present a more suspenseful and frightening description as seen through the eyes of the viewpoint character:

> A cloud of black vapor rose from the ground like smoke from a funeral pyre.

3 Direct address

Two cases of direct address remain:

> "Hey, **Tama Fook**, did you see that? Frack. What is that?"

> "Well, I'm not following it, **Greggis**. And I'm not going back to Dusa City without the satchels."

Delete the name in each case.

4 Compression

Nearly every line of dialogue that remains can and should be compressed.

This:	**Becomes:**
• "Hey, did you see that? Frack. What is that?"	• "There. Do you see that?"
• "Yes, I know it's moving. We should be quiet!"	• "I know. Quiet!"
• "Should we follow it? Or should we tell somebody what we saw?"	• "Should we follow it? Or tell someone?"
• "Well, I'm not following it ..."	• "I'm not following it ..."

5   Dialogue tags

Look at what we have so far:

> Tama Fook and his brother, Greggis, crouched behind a large granite boulder jutting from the dry earth.
>
> "There. Do you see that?"
>
> A cloud of black vapor rose from the ground like smoke from a funeral pyre. Still as the dead, the air contained not a breath of wind. Nonetheless, the mist moved. Aimlessly at first, then it turned toward the brothers and the air grew cold.
>
> Weeks of beard clung to Greggis' face in ragged, dust-clotted knots. **Horror began to mask his expression.** "It's — "
>
> "I know. Quiet!" **Tama Fook whispered, and then he hit his brother on the arm**.
>
> "Should we follow it? Or tell someone?"
>
> "I'm not following it. And I'm not going back to Dusa City without the satchels."

It's unclear who speaks the first line of dialogue. To provide action, I'll use a beat rather than using an attributive:

> "There." **Greggis pointed.** "Do you see that?"

The following line has a beat and an attributive:

> "I know. Quiet!" **Tama Fook whispered, and then he hit his brother on the arm.**

You never need both. Here, you don't need either. The previous line was spoken by Greggis. Tama Fook is the only one present to interrupt:

"I know. Quiet!"

For the same reason, the final line of the passage needs no speaker identification. Nonetheless, an appropriate gesture could make the line more emotional:

Tama Fook's callused hand cut the air with a fierce gesture. "I'm not following it. And I'm not going back to Dusa City without the satchels."

Notice that I've taken the opportunity to describe an aspect of Tama Fook: his hands.

6   Punctuation

"I know. Quiet!"

If Tama Fook wants quiet, he must not be shouting. Replace the exclamation point with a period.

7   Putting it all together

Tama Fook and his brother, Greggis, crouched behind a large granite boulder jutting from the dry earth.

"There." Greggis pointed. "Do you see that?"

A cloud of black vapor rose from the ground like smoke from a funeral pyre. Still as the dead, the air contained not a breath of wind. Nonetheless, the mist moved. Aimlessly at first, then it turned toward the brothers and the air grew cold.

Weeks of beard clung to Greggis' face in ragged, dust-clotted knots. Horror began to mask his expression. "It's — "

"I know. Quiet."

"Should we follow it? Or tell someone?"

Tama Fook's callused hand cut the air with a fierce gesture. "I'm not following it. And I'm not going back to Dusa City without the satchels."

Compare this passage with the original text at the beginning of Chapter 10. Notice how far it has come. By following the steps provided in this book, you can achieve the same effect in your writing.

Part IV

Finishing Touches

It's time to put the finishing touches on your manuscript. Because the remaining chapters focus on mechanical details rather than on the craft of writing, they don't include exercises. The hard part is over. You're in the home stretch.

14

Refining Your Manuscript

In this chapter, you'll look at the consistency of your writing style and characters throughout your manuscript; you'll check spelling, punctuation, and word usage; and you'll put your book into proper manuscript format.

Reading Out Loud

This is an important step. Don't skip it.

After making such detailed changes, does the overall flow of the text have a pleasing, easy-to-read rhythm? Find out. Read each scene out loud for sound and tone, or better yet, read it into a tape recorder and listen to the playback, or have someone else read it to you.

Pay attention to errors you make when reading out loud. Reading aloud reveals awkward passages more readily than reading silently does. You may decide to undo a few of your prose edits or make additional changes to smooth the rhythm of the text, particularly at paragraph transitions.

Character Viewpoint

Color-code your scenes by viewpoint character with colored sticky notes or highlighter pens.

For each viewpoint character, read only the scenes written from that character's point of view, preferably out loud. Make sure the character is consistent throughout the manuscript. Review your character arc table. Make sure any changes in your character's attitude are intentional and are driven by the character's arc. Correct any inconsistencies.

Character Voice

Color-code your dialogue. For each speaking character, highlight the dialogue text or underline it in a unique manner. If you have a lot of speaking characters, you may need several colors and multiple line types (single underline, double underline, thick underline, highlighted or colored text, etc.) to accomplish this. Don't color-code dialogue tags. Include only the spoken words.

Go through your manuscript once for each speaking character and read aloud only the words spoken by that character. Look for the speech mannerisms, identifying lines, language quirks, dialect, and level of sophistication you assigned to the character in Chapter 2.

Here are a few of the things I looked for in *Worlds Asunder*:

- Snider, the director of Lunar Alpha Base, rarely asks questions. He demands information.
- Chase, the investigator, is very analytical. He asks a lot of questions.
- Michelle, a student intern, is competent but not confident. She speaks hesitantly but with technical accuracy.

This step was particularly important in the case of Frank Lesperence, my especially violent character. Frank speaks with anger in every word. Because I gave him this trait after I completed my first draft, I had to make sure I hadn't missed rewriting a single line of his dialogue.

Make sure you've applied your characters' speech styles consistently throughout your manuscript. Correct any errant passages.

Pacing

Put yourself into your reader's frame of mind. Kick back with your manuscript; forget about scene structure, prose, and consistency; and read your book for fun. Enjoy the story.

Mark any place that seems too slow or moves too quickly. Don't correct anything while you're reading; you're reading for fun. Just note "slow" or "fast" in the margin and keep going.

Once you've identified the pacing problems, what can you do about them?

Sections that are too slow may suffer from any of the following problems:

1. The subject matter isn't interesting.
2. The viewpoint character doesn't have enough at stake.
3. The passage contains too much description, too much telling, or repeated information.[1]

Sections that are too fast may suffer from either of the following problems:

1. The passage is plot-driven rather than being character-driven.
2. The passage contains too much dialogue.[1]

In *Worlds Asunder,* I found a section of repeated information that I'd missed throughout the whole editing process. In short, the hook at the end of one scene revealed too much about the next scene. Even as I marked the second passage as slow, I didn't recognize it as repeated information. I figured it out later, when I looked back to determine why it seemed slow. To correct the problem, I deleted the overly revealing hook — in retrospect, the scene ending was compelling enough without it. As a result, the unchanged scene that followed no longer seemed slow.

Liabilities

I am not a lawyer and I'm not qualified to give legal advice. I will say this, however. Your manuscript may subject you to liabilities you're not aware of.

First novels, which are often autobiographical, may be particularly prone to hidden liabilities.[2] If you've fictionalized events or based your characters — even loosely — upon real people (whether you've changed the names or not), you may be at risk.

Let's say you haven't plagiarized material from another author. You haven't quoted any song lyrics, used any character or place names from other real or fictional sources, or quoted other writers. And you haven't written with malice or untruth about anybody you know or have ever heard of. So what? Even if you've done none of these things, there are other risks you need to know about.

Read *The Copyright Permission and Libel Handbook,* by Lloyd J. Jassin and Steven C. Schecter. Believe it or not, this is a quick and enjoyable read despite the subject matter. Review your manuscript for potential liabilities. If you have any doubts, consult a qualified attorney.

Style Consistency

Create a style worksheet. Divide a sheet of paper into sections and assign a few letters to each, as shown in Figure 7. Make a section for numbers and one for abbreviations and acronyms.[3] Alternatively, create a sorted electronic list. Use the worksheet to help keep your style (capitalization, hyphenation, spelling of character names and other words with alternative spellings, expression of numbers and abbreviations, etc.) consistent.

The word "email" is a good example. Should you capitalize it or not? Should you hyphenate it or not? It probably doesn't matter, but whatever you choose, be consistent.

Read through your manuscript and note your style decisions on the worksheet. Then search electronically for words that don't match your style decisions and correct them. For example, *Worlds Asunder* includes a character named Sarah (spelled with an "h"), so I searched the manuscript for "Sara" (match case, whole words only) to make sure I hadn't misspelled her name anywhere.

Commonly Misused Words

The Elements of Style, 4th Edition, by William Strunk, Jr. and E. B. White, contains an exhaustive list of commonly misused words. The list is too long to repeat here. Therefore, I refer you to *The Elements of Style* to obtain it.

A,B,C:	D,E,F:	G,H,I:	J,K,L:	M,N,O:
autopilot	data core	geo-synchronous	lift-off	
anti-missile	durapane	in-house	Lancaster	
airlock	comm link			

P,Q,R:	S,T,U:	V,W,X,Y,Z:	Numbers:	Abbreviations:
pre-flight	Situation Room	vice versa	3-D	A.M.
reassembly	Sarah	War Room	33mm	P.M.
	telnet			CATS
	thinpad			

Figure 7. Style worksheet

Search electronically for each commonly misused word. Read it in context everywhere it appears. Make sure you haven't misused it. This is a tedious process, especially with words like *this* or *than* that will appear time and again in your manuscript. Nevertheless, do this step carefully. You may be surprised, and better now than later. A profusion of misused words will get your manuscript rejected.

Other Details

See *Rewrite Right!, 2nd Edition,* by Jan Venolia, for a listing of guidelines for capitalization and expression of numbers. Search your manuscript electronically for errors and inconsistencies.

Run a grammar and spelling check. Be wary of the grammar checker provided with your word processor. Consider each passage it flags, but understand that word processors often err. Find a good grammar text and look up anything you're unsure about. Even when the checker is right, recognize that grammar conventions are looser for fiction than they are for other forms of writing. Sentence fragments, for example, are often acceptable, especially in dialogue. Any violation of the rules, though, should be deliberate and should produce a specific effect in your writing.

Manuscript Format

Always check the submission guidelines for the editor, agent, or contest you plan to submit to. If you can't find the guidelines on a website, request them via mail or email. When mailing, always include a self-addressed, stamped envelope (SASE) for the reply.

Sometimes the guidelines will be exhaustive and detailed, especially for contests. Usually, though, they specify only the format characteristics most important to the recipient. In the absence of contradictory instructions on any particular point, such as font type or margin size, use the following formatting rules.

1   All pages:
- Use 12-point Courier New or Times New Roman font.
- Double-space your manuscript, except for the address header (discussed below).
- Use the same font throughout. Don't change the font for inserts, such as letters or emails contained within your story.
- Use twenty-five lines per page, except for the first and last page of each chapter (discussed below).
- Use 1-inch margins: top, bottom, left, and right.
- Increase both right and left margins by ½ inch for inserts, such as letters or emails contained within the story.
- Do not use full justification. Leave the right-hand margin ragged.
- Do not add an extra line-space between paragraphs.
- Use a single space between sentences. Do not use two spaces after a period.
- Indent the first line of each paragraph by ½ inch.

2   First manuscript page *(see Figure 8)*:
- Type your name and address header, single-spaced, in the upper, left-hand corner.

- Type an approximate word count in the upper right-hand corner. Round this count to the nearest 5,000 words.
- Type the title in uppercase letters, centered horizontally.
- Type the word *by* one double-spaced line below the title, centered horizontally.
- Type your name one double-spaced line below the word *by*, centered horizontally.
- Type your chapter heading two double-spaced lines below your name, centered horizontally.
- Begin the text of the story two double-spaced lines below the chapter heading.
- Position the title such that nine lines of story text appear on the first page.

3   Page 2 and subsequent pages *(see Figure 9)*:
- Type the title or keyword(s), in uppercase text, in the upper-left header, ½ inch below the top of the page.
- Type your last name and the page number in the upper-right header, ½ inch below the top of the page.

4   First page of chapter 2 and subsequent chapters *(see Figure 10)*:
- Type the chapter heading on the same line as that on which the *title* appears on the first page of the manuscript, centered horizontally.
- Begin the text of the story two double-spaced lines below the chapter heading.

5   Last page *(see Figure 11)*:
- Type THE END two double-spaced lines below the last line of story text, centered horizontally.

6 Cover page *(see Figure 12)*:
- Include a cover page, formatted to match the first page of the manuscript, but without the approximate word count, chapter heading, or story text.
- If your submission is a partial manuscript, type the chapters (or pages) included, in parenthesis, two double-spaced lines below the byline, centered horizontally.
- A cover page is not the same as a cover letter. *How to Write Attention-Grabbing Query & Cover Letters,* by John Wood, contains an excellent treatment of cover and query letters, which are beyond the scope of this book.

7 Odds and ends:
- Print, single-sided, on 20-pound bond white paper (not high-gloss).
- Print with a laser printer. Ink jet printers are quickly becoming second-class.[1]
- Do not bind or staple your submission. Secure the pages with a paper clip or rubber band, depending on the size of the document.
- Do not put a copyright symbol on your submission. This is a sign of an amateur. Nobody is going to steal your book. Your copyright is protected as soon as you write your story on paper or type it into a computer, whether it has a copyright symbol on it or not.
- Do not include any artwork or illustrations.

8 Synopses:
- Manuscript formatting rules apply to a multiple-page synopsis.
- A one-page synopsis may start at the top of the page, may be single-spaced, and does not require a cover page.

Improper formatting can prompt an editor or agent to reject your manuscript without reading a single word. Take the time to format it correctly.

Proofread

Proofread carefully. Your spell checker won't catch missing words or homonyms. To catch the former, I touch each word with the tip of a pen as I read it. When my pen touches the wrong word, I know I have an error (a missing or extra word).

I can't catch homonyms for myself. Problems like *heal* in place of *heel* or *cutoff* in place of *cut off* are invisible to me. If I stop to think about it, I realize these words are wrong, but my mind knows what I'm trying to say, so it sees the correct word rather than seeing the word that's actually typed on the page. Therefore, I have somebody else proofread my work for me. I suggest you do the same.

Author's name
Author's street address
Author's city, state, and zip code
Author's phone number
Author's email address

About 85,000 words

WORLDS ASUNDER

by

Kirt Hickman

Chapter 1

"It was really embarrassing." Edward "Chase" Morgan drew the top card from the deck: the queen of diamonds. "We'd just returned from hitting a crack factory and warehouse in Cuba. This was back when President Montros thought he could stop the drug trade with air strikes."

Michelle Fairchild, Chase's materials engineering intern from Mars Tech, had won every game that evening. Not this one, though, if Chase could help it. He needed just two cards to win and Michelle hadn't lain down any of hers. Unfortunately, the queen wasn't one of the two. He put it on the discard pile.

Michelle picked it up, then placed it and two others on the table.

Chase groaned. That group put her in the lead and, at double or nothing, the credits were

Figure 8. First manuscript page

starting to add up.

She discarded a ten.

That's what Chase had been waiting for. He grabbed it, rearranged his hand, and discarded a four. "We had the weekend off before we had to fly back to Nellis, so we went out to celebrate our mission's success.

"We drank most of the night, then went to one of those all-night waffle places. They had this great-looking redheaded waitress. She was…" He stopped, unable to talk about her. Michelle was too much like a daughter to him to get into that kind of story. "Anyway, I was so busy trying to impress her, I didn't realize I'd gotten my syrup all over the place. I kept wiping it off my hands, my fork, the table, you name it. My napkin was shredded, half of it was stuck to my fingers, and no matter what I did, I just managed to make it worse."

Absently, he petted Penny, his copper-colored wiener dog, who lolled upside-down in his lap with her ears and tongue dangling toward the floor. "When I got back to my room, I found that I'd wiped my hands all down the front of my flight suit without ever realizing it."

Michelle smiled. "I can't picture you drunk."

"I haven't been drunk since I retired from the air force twenty years ago. It's your turn."

She drew a card and put it into her hand. "Did you ever ask her out?"

"The waitress? No. Whatever chance I might have had, I blew that night. I learned a few months later that the guys poured syrup on my fork handle every time I looked at her."

Michelle laughed so hard she nearly spit her coffee. "That's classic." When she recovered, she laid down a string of cards, discarding the last one. "Rummy."

"Ouch. How many is that?"

"Three."

Chase scooped up the cards and shuffled the deck together. "Sooner or later I'll win one."

Figure 9. Page 2 and subsequent pages

Chapter 2

Chase's first view of the <u>Phoenix</u> was a mere glint of sunlight on the horizon. As he drew

closer, the fuselage came into view, jutting skyward from the flat terrain like a solitary

tombstone in a garden of glittering metal. The effect gave a surreal beauty to the desolate scene.

The pod came to a stop at the boundary of the debris field. The ship was close now. The

fuselage, largely intact, rested at an odd angle at the end of a long scar in the landscape. A debris

field stretched out to the northwest, away from Chase's vehicle and the direction of the rover

tracks. Dents and cracks that marred the hull suggested that the ship had tumbled into its final

resting place. The aft section, the cargo hold, was mangled.

As it lay, the evidence was as pristine as Chase would ever see it. From here on out,

everything he did would systematically alter the reality of the scene as it had been left by the

tragedy. He ordered everyone to stay put while he took an initial look around, then stepped

outside into the oppressive heat, 110 degrees centigrade throughout the lunar day. His pressure

suit's cooling system pumped its life-sustaining fluid to maintain a safe body temperature, but the

Figure 10. First page of chapter 2 and subsequent chapters

"God willing," the president continued, "we'll never have to make them known to the worlds, let alone use the things, but I'll sleep better at night knowing they're there."

THE END

Figure 11. Last page

Author's name
Author's street address
Author's city, state, and zip code
Author's phone number
Author's email address

WORLDS ASUNDER

by

Kirt Hickman

(Chapter One through Chapter Three)

Figure 12. Cover page

15

Critiques

My first point about critiques is: You need one. Your manuscript is as good as you can make it on your own. Now it's time to get help.

Something you think is interesting might not be. Something you think is exciting might not be. Something you think is clear might not be. You're too close to your writing — you've worked on it for too long and invested too much of yourself into it — to judge it objectively. You need someone to save you from yourself.

Furthermore, even the best writing leaves opportunities for improvement that the author can't or won't catch. You owe it to your readers, and to yourself, to take advantage of those opportunities.

Professional Critiques

The methods for acquiring professional critiques vary widely in terms of cost, speed, and required effort. In general terms, you have two choices: critique groups and critique services. Whichever you choose, don't give work you haven't revised and proofed to a critiquer. If you do, the critiquer will spend her time commenting on problems you're already aware of and should have already corrected. Don't let this happen. Critiques are most valuable when they reveal the things you can't catch for yourself.

¶ Critique groups

Critique groups are generally the cheapest way, monetarily, to get your writing critiqued. They require a significant time investment, however, because you'll be expected to critique other writers' work in exchange for their critique of yours.

Working with a critique group has several benefits besides cost. It's easier to identify weaknesses in other people's writing than it is to find them in your own. Critiquing others' work will give you practice. Countless times, while revising my own fiction, I've realized: I just hammered so-and-so for making this mistake in his writing. I guess I'd better correct it in mine.

Writing is a solitary venture. Critique groups provide an opportunity to meet with people who share your passion and to talk with them about writing. It's a great way to learn about upcoming contests or agents who are actively seeking your kind of story.

The only downside is, if you need to have your complete manuscript critiqued, the amount of time it takes to get through it will depend on how often your group meets and the permitted submission size.

To save time, go though the revisions discussed in Chapters 1 through 8 of this book. Then work on the rest of the revision process, Chapters 9 through 14, one scene or chapter at a time. This way, you can receive feedback on the early, polished pages while you're still revising later pages.

Another potential problem with many critique groups is that their members are amateur writers and critiquers. You may be leery of receiving bad advice, but in my experience, this isn't a problem. Different members will have different strengths. Each is more likely to comment within his areas of strength rather than in his areas of weakness. Because you'll get separate critiques from each member, there's a good chance that the group as a whole will correctly identify your writing weaknesses.

Look for critique groups on-line or check with your local writers' clubs for leads on critique groups near you.

2 Critique services

Critique services are usually the quickest, most expensive way to get a critique. If you want professional feedback quickly and have the money to pay for it, this may be an option for you. Check with your local writer's clubs or search on-line for these services. Prices vary widely, so shop around. I use the service offered through SouthWest Writers at www.southwestwriters.com.

Test Readers

In addition to getting a professional critique, give your manuscript to at least two readers of your genre who are *not* professional writers. You want someone to look at your book from the perspective of a reader. Ask them to evaluate your manuscript for pacing and other obvious problems. Specifically, have them identify:

1 Sections that seem to move too quickly.
2 Sections that seem to drag or are boring.
3 Sections they have difficulty following (anything that doesn't make sense, whether it's the meaning of a sentence, the motivation of a character, a technical explanation, or whatever).
4 Any other happen-to-see problems.

Have each reader mark where he stops reading any time he puts the book down. It may mean nothing. It may be that his lunch break ended and he had to go back to work, but if all your readers set the book down in the same place, look for a problem there, even if none of them noted one.

Ask each reader how he liked the story. Could he relate to the hero? Expect vague responses, like:

Empathy is building slowly with the main character, I'm not
sure why.

Remember, these people aren't professional writers and critiquers. They may not articulate specific solutions. Nevertheless,
value their opinions; they represent your potential market.

Select readers you can trust to give honest feedback. If someone hands back your manuscript and says, "It was great. I loved
it," and offers no criticism, be afraid. Either this person is not being honest, or he's not being objective. Give your manuscript to
someone else and get another opinion. I've said this before, but
it bears repeating. Even the best writing leaves opportunities for
improvement. You owe it to yourself and to your reader to take
advantage of those opportunities.

For *Worlds Asunder*, I had seven test readers and two professional critiques. By the time the manuscript was ready for its second
critique, I had no illusions. I knew my writing, and my story, had
weaknesses. I wanted them purged.

Accepting Criticism

Accepting feedback, especially critical feedback (the kind your
critiquer is supposed to give you), can be difficult. You worked
hard on your story. You poured your heart and soul, not to mention many hours of your life, into it. Having someone criticize it
can be devastating.

Keep these important things in mind as you listen to, or read,
your critiquer's comments. First, they're not personal. They're
intended to make your writing better. Your critiquer is genuinely trying to help you. Second, you asked for, and possibly paid
for, her *honest* opinion. Don't get upset when she gives it to you.
Third, no matter what problems she finds, you can correct them,
and the result will be well worth the effort.

When I got back my first critique of *Worlds Asunder* (Chapters
1 through 5), I was crushed. I'd never received feedback on my
writing and I thought it was wonderful. It wasn't. It was awful. I
received negative remarks spanning nearly every topic discussed

in *Revising Fiction*. My critiquer wasn't being vindictive. She was being honest. Nevertheless, I threw her critique onto the counter and gave up writing.

Two hours later, something — masochism, maybe — compelled me to pick up that critique and read the whole thing again. This time, I wasn't surprised by what it said. I read it more objectively and something amazing happened. As I read comment after comment, criticism after criticism, I realized my critiquer was right. For nearly every problem, once she mentioned it, I could see it. I thought if I could recognize the problems when she pointed them out, I could probably learn to find them for myself.

I read the rest of *Worlds Asunder* and concluded that the writing improved as the manuscript progressed. I needed confirmation, so I asked the same critiquer to comment on the rest of the manuscript. I was right. According to her, it got better in Chapter 7 and better still in Chapter 10. I embarked then on a mission to learn how to revise, a journey that taught me everything I've written in this book. The example passages you've read illustrate the impact this journey has had on my writing. As a sign of my appreciation, I've dedicated *Revising Fiction* to Eileen Stanton, the woman who wrote that first critique.

If you receive spoken rather than written feedback, it's easy — even natural — to defend your work. Don't. If you justify your writing with statements like, "The reason I did that was…" or "I disagree because…" you'll shut down your critiquer. He doesn't care why you wrote your story the way you did; he's just stating his observations. Whether you agree with his comments or not, say, "Thank you." Doing so will keep the feedback coming. After all, that's what you're there for. In the end, if you disagree with this or that particular comment, don't make changes based on it.

Do ask questions to clarify your critiquer's comments, questions like: "Can you give me an example?" or "Do you think it would help if I made this change?" These kinds of questions are productive. They show the critiquer that you're listening and that you welcome his feedback. And his answers will help you make the appropriate revisions.

Rewrite

You're likely to get a wide range of comments from your critiquers and test readers, everything from, "It's great. I loved it," to "It's awful. I hated it." You'll get contradictory feedback on specific issues. When I asked two writing friends of mine, Keith Pyeatt and David J. Corwell, to critique the same twenty-page excerpt from an early draft of *Venus Rain*, Keith wrote:

> "La Roche comes across as a very intelligent man. Great job with his character. I love good, highly developed gray characters, so I'm really enjoying La Roche."

David wrote:

> "The character that least worked for me was La Roche ... He didn't feel developed enough."

While Keith sounds like he's just being gracious, he criticized many other aspects of the story. Therefore, I believe he was being honest. This example shows that different people have different tastes and expectations. You can't please them all.

So what do you do with contradictory feedback? First, recognize that whatever other people think, *you* are the author. Only you can decide what works for you and for your story. Having said that, consider each comment carefully before you decide whether to accept or discard it. Recognize that you do *not* have an objective viewpoint.

Here's my rule of thumb: Get feedback from as many sources as possible. If two critiquers or test readers mark something as a problem, it warrants some change. I also consider comments that come from only one source. Often, I agree with them. Mine becomes the second condemning opinion and I change the passage.

Revise the New Passages

Once you've rewritten a scene, paragraph, or even a single word of your manuscript, you must give the changes the same level of scrutiny you gave your first draft writing.

If you write a new scene:

1. Make a scene card (Chapter 4) and look for gross problems (Chapter 6).
2. Consider manuscript organization (Chapter 6) when deciding where to insert the scene.
3. Consider whether the new scene affects your chapter numbering (Chapter 7).
4. Make sure you haven't repeated information from another scene (Chapter 8).
5. Revise the scene (Chapter 9).

For all new text, including new scenes, paragraphs, sentences, and even individual words:

1. Polish your prose and dialogue (Chapters 11 & 12).
2. Look for violations of your style decisions (Chapter 14).
3. Run a grammar and spelling check.

Final Proof

Proof your work. You will submit this draft of your manuscript to editors and literary agents. Typographical, grammatical, and other errors will tell them you don't take your writing seriously. This is probably an unfair assessment. If you've spent the time and effort to do the revisions prescribed in this book, you obviously take your writing seriously. You're just too close to the project to catch your own mistakes. Don't let that keep you from being published after you've worked so hard.

Have someone else, someone qualified, proof it for you. Pay him if you have to. If he's a professional editor or proofreader, he's worth the expense. When I started paying a proofreader to go over my work, I began placing in contests and getting positive replies from editors and agents. Prior to that, I received nothing but rejections. Don't underestimate the power of proofreading.

Celebrate and Submit

Congratulations! You've finished your book. It's time to celebrate and submit, in that order. The submission process is long, arduous, and beyond the scope of this book. I will, however, offer a word of advice: Endure.

It may take months to hear back about your submissions. A literary agency once asked for sample chapters of *Worlds Asunder* three years after I sent my query letter. Furthermore, you'll probably get many, many rejections before you receive a single positive response. Don't sit by your phone, computer, or mailbox. Begin your next writing project. The time will pass quickly while you're busy. The replies will come.

Notes

Chapter 2

1. See also Nancy Kress. *Characters, Emotion & Viewpoint*. Writer's Digest Books. 2005.

Chapter 3

1. Joseph Campbell. *The Hero with a Thousand Faces*. Princeton University Press. 1973.
2. Christopher Vogler. *The Writer's Journey: Mythic Structure for Writers, 2nd Edition*. Michael Wiese Productions. 1998.

Chapter 4

1. Tom Bird. ~~Write~~ *Right from God*. Sojourn, Inc. 2003.
2. Adapted from a similar scene card described by Raymond Obstfeld. *Novelist's Essential Guide to Crafting Scenes*. Writer's Digest Books. 2000.

Chapter 6

1. Sol Stein. *Stein on Writing*. St. Martin's Griffin. 2000.

Chapter 9

1. See also Noah Lukeman. *The First Five Pages*. Simon & Schuster. 2000.
2. Raymond Obstfeld. *Novelist's Essential Guide to Crafting Scenes*. Writer's Digest Books. 2000.
3. Sol Stein. *Stein on Writing*. St. Martin's Griffin. 2000.

Chapter 11

1. William Strunk, Jr. and E. B. White. *The Elements of Style, 4th Edition*. Longman Publishing Group. 1999.
2. Noah Lukeman. *The First Five Pages*. Simon & Schuster. 2000.
3. Expanded from a list provided by Jan Venolia. *Rewright Right!, 2nd Edition*. Ten Speed Press. 2000.
4. See also Noah Lukeman. *The First Five Pages*. Simon & Schuster. 2000.

Chapter 12

1. Renni Browne & Dave King. *Self-Editing for Fiction Writers, 2nd Edition*. HarperCollins. 2004.

Chapter 14

1. See also Noah Lukeman. *The First Five Pages*. Simon & Schuster. 2000.
2. Lloyd J. Jassin and Steven C. Schecter. *The Copyright Permission and Libel Handbook*. John Wiley & Sons, Inc. 1998.
3. Jan Venolia. *Rewrite Right!, 2nd Edition*. Ten Speed Press. 2000.

Self-Editing Checklist

Your concept: P, 2O
- ☐ Determine your theme 2O
- ☐ Build your world, including: 2O
  - Physical world
  - Moral codes
  - Economics
  - Domestic politics
  - World politics
  - Religion
  - Paranormal elements (if any)
  - Scientific advancement
  - Day-to-day life (How does it differ from the here and now?)
  - All must mesh into a coherent whole

Characters: P.25
- ☐ Determine the following for each major character: 26
  - Physical traits
  - Style of speech
  - Character flaws
  - Special skill
  - Definable personality
  - Identifying lines, mannerisms, and props
  - Virtues
  - Backstory
  - Know how the character will change throughout the story
- ☐ Check for characterization pitfalls: 36
  - Make sure each character has a unique personality
  - Make your hero strong-willed
  - Remove clichéd character traits
  - Don't forget your secondary characters
- ☐ Fill out a character profile for each character 41

Plot: P.45
- ☐ Verify the plot basics
  - Make sure you have a hero the reader will care about
  - Give your hero a noble goal
  - Make the stakes high
  - Put a difficult obstacle in your hero's way
  - Make sure your hero performs the action most responsible for resolving the central conflict

- • Make your hero go through a life-altering change
- • Make sure you haven't lost the thread of cause and effect anywhere in your manuscript
- ❑ Include each checkpoint of the mythic structure 46
  - • Ordinary life
  - • Story starting point
  - • Heeding the call
  - • Allies and enemies
  - • Approaching the dark moment
  - • Dark moment
  - • Return
  - • Climax
  - • Permanence of the change
- ❑ Build suspense 53
  - • Make at least one character especially violent or adversarial
  - • Spring surprises
  - • Mislead your reader
  - • Do your worst
  - • Take away that which is most important to your hero
  - • Haunt your hero with memories of a past failure
  - • Turn the environment loose upon your characters
  - • Employ phobias
  - • Never make anything easy
  - • Show that the danger is real
  - • Impose a deadline
  - • Prevent your hero from running away
  - • Include a final twist near the end
  - • Use these techniques in combination
- ❑ Make a character-arc table 63

First Draft (do the following for each scene): P. 68
- ❑ Select a viewpoint character
- ❑ Make a setting card
- ❑ Write the scene
- ❑ Make a scene card

Research: P. 81
- ❑ Do the research

Gross problems: P. 85
- ❑ Go through your scene cards (take notes on the back of each card)

- Make sure each scene develops character and/or advances the plot
- Eliminate any "puppet" scenes
- Add action and conflict to static conversations
- Organize the scenes in your manuscript
- Check your characters' arcs
- Resolve any inconsistencies
- Resolve each suspense element

❑ Develop your opening scene 89
❑ Enhance your setting 91
❑ Rewrite your scenes (or write new ones) to correct the problems identified above 93

Chapters: P. 97
❑ Evaluate your prologue (if applicable)
❑ Define your chapters breaks

Exposition: P. 105
❑ Eliminate information dumps
❑ Relocate misplaced information
❑ Eliminate repeated information
❑ Make sure you've revealed your characters gradually through their thoughts, actions, emotions, and dialogue

Scenes (do the following for each scene): P. 123
❑ Evaluate the scene structure
❑ Develop the scene opening
❑ Convert *tell* to *show*
❑ Look for emotions that are told instead of shown
❑ Eliminate anachronistic scene content
❑ Develop the scene ending
❑ Eliminate digressions
❑ Evaluate the scene's length
❑ Edit the scene to build tension
❑ Make sure you've revealed your setting in an effective way
❑ Eliminate viewpoint violations
❑ Make sure each character is consistent throughout the manuscript
❑ Make sure you've described your characters in a effective way
❑ Examine your characterization, including:
  - Describe your characters in a way that evokes emotion
  - Limit ways of referring to newly introduced characters
  - Don't introduce unimportant characters by name
  - Don't introduce too many characters at once

Prose: *P. 176*

- ☐ Minimize your use of to-be verbs
- ☐ Minimize your use of as-ing sentences
- ☐ Eliminate filter words
- ☐ Eliminate thinker attributives
- ☐ Eliminate italics used for direct thoughts wherever possible
- ☐ Look for opportunities to use comparisons
- ☐ Increase specificity
- ☐ Consider your verb choice
- ☐ Minimize *not* and the contraction *n't*
- ☐ Eliminate unnecessary uses of the word *that*
- ☐ Eliminate clichés
- ☐ Eliminate repeated elements
- ☐ Minimize your use of repeated sentence beginnings and other repeated words
- ☐ Eliminate unnecessary adverbs
- ☐ Eliminate unnecessary and unimaginative adjectives
- ☐ Eliminate unnecessary prepositional phrases
- ☐ Eliminate anachronistic words and phrases
- ☐ Rewrite expressions that can be written with fewer words
- ☐ Make sure every pronoun has a clear and correct antecedent
- ☐ Minimize the questions that appear in your character's thoughts
- ☐ Look for ways to enhance subtlety
- ☐ Make sure the meaning of every sentence and phrase is clear
- ☐ Make sure your verb tense is consistent
- ☐ Evaluate your paragraph breaks
- ☐ Correct punctuation errors

Dialogue: *P. 215*

- ☐ Eliminate everyday dialogue
- ☐ Eliminate informative dialogue
- ☐ Eliminate direct address
- ☐ Eliminate self-talk dialogue
- ☐ Compress your dialogue
- ☐ Minimize your use of non-*said* attributives
- ☐ Eliminate verb-first attributives
- ☐ Make sure the dialogue matches the actions and emotions of the speaker
- ☐ Edit out long words in dialogue unless they're right for the character
- ☐ Look for opportunities to use contractions
- ☐ Use run-on sentences and sentence fragments to emulate speech patterns

❏ Eliminate melodramatic dialogue
❏ Minimize your use of phonetic spellings
❏ Separate your paragraphs by speaker
❏ Evaluate your dialogue tags for:
  • Tags that are in the wrong place
  • Too few tags
  • Too many tags
  • Repetitive tags
❏ Eliminate tags that explain dialogue content
❏ Eliminate dialogue tags that tell emotion
❏ Correct punctuation errors
❏ Read the dialogue out loud for sound and pacing

Refining Your Manuscript: P ᒐᕁᕁ
❏ Read each scene out loud
❏ Make sure each character's viewpoint is consistent
❏ Make sure each character's voice is consistent
❏ Read your manuscript for pacing
❏ Review your manuscript for legal liabilities
❏ Read your manuscript for inconsistent style decisions and create a style worksheet
❏ Search electronically for words that don't match your style decisions and correct them
❏ Search electronically for commonly misused words and make sure you haven't misused them
❏ Make sure your capitalization and expression of numbers are correct and consistent
❏ Run a spelling and grammar check
❏ Format your manuscript
❏ Proofread your manuscript

Critiques: p·2⁹1
❏ Have your manuscript critiqued
❏ Have at least two test readers read your manuscript
❏ Rewrite your manuscript based on critique and test-reader feedback
❏ Revise the rewritten portions
❏ Do a final proof
❏ Celebrate and submit

Bibliography

1. Andrew Adamson, Vicky Jenson. *Shrek.* Dreamworks. 2003.
2. James Scott Bell. *Plot & Structure.* Writer's Digest Books. 2004.
3. Tom Bird. ~~Write~~ *Right from God.* Sojourn, Inc. 2003.
4. Renni Browne and Dave King. *Self-Editing for Fiction Writers, 2nd Edition.* HarperCollins. 2004.
5. Tom Chiarella. *Writing Dialogue.* Story Press. 1998.
6. Tami D. Cowden, Caro LaFever, Sue Viders. *The Complete Writer's Guide to Heroes & Heroines: Sixteen Master Archetypes.* Lone Eagle Publishing Company. 2000.
7. Nora Ephron. *You've Got Mail.* Warner Bros. 1998.
8. James N. Frey. *How to Write a Damn Good Novel.* St. Martin's Press. 1987.
9. Ann Hood. *Creating Character Emotions.* Story Press. 1998.
10. Lloyd J. Jassin and Steven C. Schecter. *The Copyright Permission and Libel Handbook.* John Wiley & Sons, Inc. 1998.
11. Stephen King. *On Writing.* Pocket Books. 2000.
12. Nancy Kress. *Characters, Emotion & Viewpoint.* Writer's Digest Books. 2005.
13. Nancy Kress. *Dynamic Characters.* Writers Digest Books. 2004.
14. *New American Standard Bible.* The Lockman Foundation. 1995.
15. Noah Lukeman. *The First Five Pages.* Simon & Schuster. 2000.
16. Mary Lynn. *Every Page Perfect, 4th Edition.* Lynnx Ink. 2001.
17. Merriam-Webster. *The Merriam-Webster Dictionary.* Pocket Books. 1974.
18. Merriam-Webster. *Merriam-Webster's Pocket Guide to Punctuation, 2nd Edition.* Merriam-Webster, Incorporated. 2001.
19. *The Holy Bible, New Century Version.* Thomas Nelson, Inc. 2005.
20. Raymond Obstfeld. *Novelist's Essential Guide to Crafting Scenes, 2nd Edition.* Writer's Digest Books. 2000.
21. Eugene H. Peterson. *The Message: The Bible in Contemporary Language.* NavPress Publishing Group. 2002.
22. J. I. Rodale and Nancy LaRoche. *The Synonym Finder.* Warner Books. 1978.
23. Ron Rozelle. *Description & Setting.* Writer's Digest Books. 2005.
24. Steven Spielberg. *Raiders of the Lost Ark.* Paramount Pictures. 1981.
25. Eileen Stanton. "Ten Ways to Create Interesting Characters." Unpublished.
26. Sol Stein. *Stein on Writing.* St. Martin's Griffin. 2000.
27. William Strunk, Jr. and E. B. White. *The Elements of Style, 4th Edition.* Longman Publishing Group. 1999.
28. Jan Venolia. *Rewrite Right!, 2nd Edition.* Ten Speed Press. 2000.
29. Christopher Vogler. *The Writer's Journey: Mythic Structure for Writers, 2nd Edition.* Michael Wiese Productions. 1998.
30. John Wood. *How to Write Attention-Grabbing Query & Cover Letters.* Writer's Digest Books. 1996.

Index

Murder was only the beginning…

Edward "Chase" Morgan, NASA's accident investigator at Lunar Alpha Base, plans an uneventful retirement — until the crash of the Stellarfare *Phoenix* kills the United States Secretary of Energy and turns Chase's last case into a fight to avert war. Evidence of deliberate sabotage and Chinese government involvement suggest that this is the first in a series of political moves designed to undermine America's interplanetary clout. Events escalate as both sides break decades-old treaties. But when Chase learns that someone fabricated the evidence, he suspects conspiracy. Now he must find proof before the expanding crisis tears all of the colonized worlds asunder

Review:

As a kid, I was addicted to science fiction. From Tom Swift to Isaac Asimov, Robert A. Heinlein and Ray Bradbury, I devoured them all. I even took a sci-fi lit course in college. But apart from a brief return to the genre in the '80s for Margaret Atwood's *The Handmaid's Tale*, it's been 30 years since I've read any science fiction. I just wasn't into it.

Kirt Hickman's debut novel, *Worlds Asunder,* may have cured me of my indifference. Or perhaps it's just created a new addiction: to Hickman's storytelling.

The science in *Worlds Asunder* is credible and, given Hickman's engineering background, probably accurate. But it's the fiction side of the "science fiction" label that kept me wanting more. Clean, clear and compelling, Hickman's action-packed story gripped me from the first page and didn't release me until its satisfying conclusion 260 pages later.

Worlds Asunder is a great read—whether you're a sci-fi aficionado or just like a first-class story. I'm looking forward to whatever Hickman comes up with next.

– Mark David Gerson
   award winning author of *The MoonQuest: A True Fantasy* and
   The Voice of the Muse: Answering the Call to Write

Available at quillrunner.com
ISBN: 978-0-9796330-0-3 (Hardcover) ISBN: 978-0-9796330-2-7 (Paperback)

About the Author

Kirt Hickman, author of the 2008 science-fiction conspiracy thriller *Worlds Asunder,* was born in Albuquerque, New Mexico in 1966. Kirt was a technical writer for fourteen years before branching into fiction. During his technical career, he made a living out of taking complex sets of requirements, or in this case advice, and boiling them down into simple, effective procedures. His methodical approach to self-editing has helped many make sense of the mass of advice available to the novice writer. He teaches self-editing classes through SouthWest Writers. He has been a mentor in the SWW mentoring program, has spoken at several conferences, and contributes a monthly column titled "Revising Fiction" to the SouthWest Sage.

Printed in the United States
220282BV00004B/2/P